Darlyn

I hope this book will in some small way help you through the bad times Stay close to the Lord and always remember I'm here too.

Love
Mary Lynn

WOMAN

Spencer W. Kimball

N. Eldon Tanner

Marion G. Romney

Ezra Taft Benson

Mark E. Petersen

LeGrand Richards

Boyd K. Packer

Marvin J. Ashton

Bruce R. McConkie

David B. Haight

Neal A. Maxwell

Marion D. Hanks

Rex D. Pinegar

G. Homer Durham

James M. Paramore

WOMAN

Deseret Book Company
Salt Lake City, Utah
1980

CONTENTS

FOREWORD   *Barbara B. Smith*
Page vii

INTRODUCTION   *President*
Page 1   *Spencer W. Kimball*

NO GREATER HONOR: *President*
THE WOMAN'S ROLE   *N. Eldon Tanner*
Page 4

WOMAN AS MOTHER   *Elder*
Page 13   *David B. Haight*

WOMAN AS A TEACHER   *Elder*
Page 21   *Rex D. Pinegar*

WOMAN'S RESPONSIBILITY   *Elder*
TO LEARN   *G. Homer Durham*
Page 32

THE ETERNAL   *Elder*
COMPANIONSHIP: *LeGrand Richards*
HUSBAND AND WIFE
Page 41

WOMAN'S RELATIONSHIP TO   *Elder*
THE PRIESTHOOD   *James M. Paramore*
Page 46

EVE AND THE FALL   *Elder*
Page 57   *Bruce R. McConkie*

TO THE ELECT WOMEN OF   *President*
THE KINGDOM OF GOD   *Ezra Taft Benson*
Page 69

THE BLESSINGS AND   *President*
RESPONSIBILITIES OF   *Spencer W. Kimball*
WOMANHOOD
Page 77

WOMAN'S ROLE IN THE
COMMUNITY
Page 86

Elder
Marvin J. Ashton

THE WOMEN OF GOD
Page 94

Elder
Neal A. Maxwell

"MAGIC APLENTY"
Page 99

Elder
Marion D. Hanks

WHY EVERY WOMAN NEEDS
RELIEF SOCIETY
Page 123

Elder
Mark E. Petersen

BEGIN WHERE YOU ARE—
AT HOME
Page 131

Elder
Boyd K. Packer

SCRIPTURES AND
FAMILY STABILITY
Page 140

President
Marion G. Romney

INDEX
Page 149

FOREWORD

By Barbara B. Smith
Relief Society General President

Each year, hundreds of pieces of mail come to my desk from all parts of the world. Some are statements of platforms about new goals for women; some are cries for help from individual sisters who do not understand clearly what the Lord expects of them; a few are angry statements from sisters who have been hurt or treated unfairly; some are questions about the role of women in today's world. These letters indicate to me that the woman of today faces challenges and opportunities unheard of in her grandmother's time, and the changing world brings with it a host of new and perplexing problems. I am becoming increasingly aware of the need to consider these problems in the light of gospel principles.

The book *Woman* brings important spiritual perspective to a number of concerns that lie close to the heart of every daughter of God. Herein is found the vital message that our Father in heaven cares about us—that he wants women to be fulfilled and happy and important and worthwhile. Here are answers to so many of the questions that trouble women, especially LDS women, in these latter days.

I am especially gratified that this book offers dignity and recognition to the divine occupation of motherhood, an occupation that the world tends to shun as being unrewarding and unfulfilling. The counsel to single women brought forth here is also particularly timely and valuable. There are words of help, of hope, of eternal value for women in virtually every aspect of their existence, and the underlying tone is one of respect for the scope of woman's influence and the power she has to improve our world.

Ours is a most exciting age—an age in which women have more time, more opportunity, and more inclination to use their creative talents to the utmost. But with so many exciting possibilities clamoring for our attention, it becomes difficult to separate those which will give only momentary satisfaction from those which offer eternal blessings. I'm grateful for the guidance of prophets to help me discern where I can most profitably put my creative energies to work.

All of us, male and female, must use our talents in every way we can, because it will take the best that is in each of us to make headway in solving the problems of the world today. And perhaps more important for us, it will take all our heart, might, mind, and strength to do the work the Lord has given us—that is, to live so that we, and those we can influence, will gain exaltation in the kingdom of God. This special book will help not only to keep us on the right road, but also to understand what a beautiful and sacred road it is we travel.

WOMAN

INTRODUCTION

President Spencer W. Kimball

It is fitting that a book on the subject of women be published at this time. There has never been a time in the world when the role of woman has been more confused. There has never been a time in the Church when women are able to do more to show what their true role in the world can and ought to be. The impact and influence of women and mothers on our world is most important. The thought that "the hand that rocks the cradle rules the world" is more viable today than ever before.

There are many important women in the life of every person born to this mortal existence. I think of the spirit of revelation that my own dear wife invites into our home because of the hours she has spent every year of our married life in studying the scriptures, so that she can be prepared to teach the principles of the gospel. I think of the sweet and tender spirit that accompanies her after she spends her time in compassionate service or in loving fellowship as a visiting teacher. Our sisters acknowledge by their deeds their willingness to follow the Savior and to make sacrifices for the kingdom of God. They strengthen each other as they grow and learn together. They share their testimonies about the magnitude of their callings to care for others and their knowledge that the Lord aids them as they seek help with those responsibilities.

I marvel at the faithfulness of so many of our sisters and their unswerving devotion to the cause of righteousness. My own wonderful mother's journal records a lifetime of being grateful for the opportunity to serve, and of feeling regretful only that she couldn't do more. I smiled when I recently read one entry, dated January 16, 1900.

She was serving as first counselor in the Relief Society presidency in Thatcher, Arizona, and the presidency went to a sister's home where caring for a sick baby had kept the mother from doing her sewing. Mother took her own sewing machine, a picnic lunch, her baby, and a high chair, and they began work. She wrote that night that they had "made four aprons, four pairs of pants and started a shirt for one of the boys." They had to stop at four o'clock to go to a funeral, so they "did not get any more than that done." I would have been impressed by such an achievement, rather than thinking, "Well, that's not much."

That's the kind of home into which I was born, one conducted by a woman who breathed service in all her actions. That is the kind of home my wife has made. That is the kind of home that thousands of wonderful women all over the Church make for their husbands and children, and I firmly feel that much of that success rests in the ideals of the gospel of Jesus Christ.

It is a great blessing to be a woman in the Church today. The opposition against righteousness has never been greater, but the opportunities for fulfilling our highest potential have also never been greater.

What is our greatest potential? Is it not to achieve godhood ourselves? What are the qualities we must develop to achieve such greatness? Many of these qualities are discussed in this wonderful volume, such as intelligence, light, and knowledge. What special opportunities do women have for such development? These qualities, you will remember, are part of the promise given to the sisters by the Prophet Joseph Smith. Since we learn best by teaching others, our sisters may see the fulfillment of that promise daily as they teach children at home, in Sunday School, and in Primary; as they teach in the Relief Society; as they participate in sacrament meetings; and in their daily conversation. We urge those who are called to teach to magnify their callings through study and prayer, recognizing the eternal values they are building for themselves as well as for those whom they teach. We encourage all our sisters to take advantage of their opportunities to receive light and knowledge in school, in personal study, and in Relief Society.

Another important quality is leadership. Women have unique opportunities to grow in leadership skills. Do we think of leadership as telling others what to do, or as making all the decisions? We do not. Leadership is the ability to encourage the best efforts of others in working toward a desirable goal. Who has more significant opportunities to lead than a mother who guides her children toward perfection, or the wife who daily counsels with her husband, that they may grow together? The tremendous contribution in leadership made by women in the auxiliaries of the Church and in their communities is likewise beyond measure.

Perhaps the most essential godlike quality is compassion—compassion that is shown in unselfish service to others, that ultimate expression of concern for others that we call love. The Church provides women with special opportunities to express their feelings of charity, benevolence, and love. There are other avenues of service also, in the community and especially in the home. Wherever women are true to their feminine natures and magnify their opportunities for loving service, they are learning to become more like God.

I have mentioned only a few of the special blessings God gives his daughters in helping them to become like him. This volume is full of counsel and teachings from men chosen by the Lord to lead his children. May our sisters in the gospel be blessed by these words and grow to the full flowering of their potential as we help each other along the path to perfection.

NO GREATER HONOR: THE WOMAN'S ROLE

President N. Eldon Tanner

In this church we have a great body of wonderful women—wives, mothers, and single women engaged in the work of the Lord and in the service of their fellowmen. They are affiliated with the Relief Society, the principal woman's organization; the Primary, where our children are instructed; the Sunday School, where the gospel is taught to all members; the Mutual, which is the activity and social organization for youth and adults; and our women serve with dedication and skill in various other capacities.

After I had discussed business matters with some men one day, the conversation took on a more personal, informal note when one man said, "I have the most wonderful wife in the world." Another said, "That's what *you* think. I think *I* have the best." A third man said, "Isn't it a great blessing to have a wife you love, who loves you, one who is a good mother and homemaker, who has high ideals, who believes in God and wants to help her family accept and live the teachings of the gospel of Jesus Christ?"

What woman could want any greater glory or tribute than that which comes from an appreciative and loving husband? The applause and homage of the world fade into insignificance when compared with the approbation of God and expressions of love and appreciation that come from the hearts and lips of those who are nearest and dearest to her.

From the beginning God has made it clear that woman is very special, and he has also very clearly defined her position, her duties, and her destiny in the divine plan. One of her greatest privileges, blessings, and opportunities is to be a co-partner with God in bringing his spirit children into the world.

4

It is of great concern to all who understand this glorious concept that Satan and his cohorts are using scientific arguments and nefarious propaganda to lure women away from their primary responsibilities as wives, mothers, and homemakers. We hear so much about emancipation, independence, sexual liberation, birth control, abortion, and other insidious propaganda belittling the role of motherhood, all of which is Satan's way of destroying woman, the home, and the family—the basic unit of society.

Some effective tools include the use of radio, television, and magazines, where pornography abounds and where women are being debased and disgracefully used as sex symbols—sex-ploited, some call it. Immodest dress, drugs, and alcohol daily take a tremendous toll through the destruction of virtue and chastity and even lives. With modern electronic devices of communication and speedy transportation, much more is being heard throughout the world by many more people than would be possible otherwise, and it is having its degrading influence and effect.

Yes, pornography, drugs, and alcohol are available to young and old in alarming quantity, and are destroying the moral values and further deteriorating the minds and thought processes of those who succumb to these devilish wiles.

President Dallin Oaks recently said to the student body at Brigham Young University, "We are surrounded by the promotional literature of illicit sexual relations on the printed page and on the screen. For your own good, avoid it. Pornographic or erotic stories and pictures are worse than filthy or polluted food. The body has defenses to rid itself of unwholesome food, but the brain won't vomit back filth. Once recorded it will always remain subject to recall, flashing its perverted images across your mind, and drawing you away from the wholesome things in life."

It is so important that our young girls keep

themselves from this kind of pollution. The girls of today will be the women of tomorrow, and it is necessary that they prepare for that role. Can you imagine the kind of world we will have in the future if the girls of today are weakened morally to the extent that virtue will not be taught in their homes, and if any children they might have are not nurtured within the walls of homes sanctified by the holy laws of matrimony?

Marriage is ordained of God, and we must do everything we can to strengthen the ties that bind, to strengthen our homes, and to prepare ourselves by exemplary living to teach our children the ways of God, which is the only way for them to find happiness here and eternal life hereafter.

As we enumerate the many important responsibilities a woman has in connection with her duties as a wife, a mother, a homemaker, a sister, a sweetheart, or a good neighbor, it should be evident that these challenging responsibilities can satisfy her need to express her talents, her interests, her creativity, dedication, energy, and skills, which so many seek to satisfy outside the home. It is impossible to estimate the lasting influence for good a woman can have in any of these roles. Let me remind us all of her primary responsibilities.

First of all, as I mentioned before, she is a co-partner with God in bringing his spirit children into the world. What a glorious concept! No greater honor could be given. With this honor comes the tremendous responsibility of living and caring for those children so they might learn their duty as citizens and what they must do to return to their Heavenly Father. They must be taught to understand the gospel of Jesus Christ and to accept and live his teachings. As they understand the purpose of life, why they are here and where they are going, they will have a reason for choosing the right and avoiding the temptations and buffetings of Satan, who is so very real and determined to destroy them.

A mother has far greater influence on her children

than anyone else has, and she must realize that every word she speaks, every act, every response, her attitude, even her appearance and manner of dress, affect the lives of her children and the whole family. It is while the child is in the home that he gains from his mother the attitudes, hopes, and beliefs that will determine the kind of life he will live and the contribution he will make to society.

President Brigham Young expressed the thought that mothers are the moving instruments in the hands of Providence and are the machinery that give zest to the whole man, and guide the destinies and lives of men and nations upon the earth. He further said, "Let mothers of any nation teach their children not to make war, and the children would not grow up and enter into it." (*Journal of Discourses* 19:72.)

It is interesting to note that when executives of companies look for new employees or are planning promotions for their experienced ones, they always want to know what kind of wife a man has. This seems to be very important. In the Church when men are being considered for new priesthood offices, the question is always raised about the worthiness of the wife and whether or not she can give him full support.

Women, you are of great strength and support to the men in your lives, and they sometimes need your help most when they are least deserving. A man can have no greater incentive, no greater hope, no greater strength than to know that his mother, his sweetheart, or his wife has confidence in him and loves him. And a man should strive every day to live worthy of that love and confidence.

President Hugh B. Brown once said at a Relief Society conference: "There are people fond of saying that women are the weaker instruments, but I don't believe it. Physically they may be, but spiritually, morally, religiously, and in faith, what man can match a woman who is really converted to the gospel! Women are more will-

ing to make sacrifices than are men, more patient in
suffering, more earnest in prayer. They are the peers and
often superior to men in resilience, in goodness, in morality, and in faith." (September 29, 1965.)

And girls, don't underestimate your influence on
your brothers and your sweethearts. As you live worthy
of their love and respect you can help greatly to determine that they will be clean and virtuous, successful
and happy. Always remember that you can go much
further on respect than on popularity. I was reading the
other day of a report of a conversation between two
young prisoners of war. One said, "I am sick of war,
bombers, destruction, prison camps, and everything and
everybody." "I feel much like that myself," said the other.
"But there is a girl back home who is praying that I will
come back. She cares, and it really helps me endure all
these atrocities."

To mothers, daughters, and women everywhere, let
me stress the fact that because of your great potential and
influence for good in the lives of all of us, Satan is determined to destroy you. You cannot compromise with
him. You must have the courage, the strength, the desire,
and the determination to live as the Lord would have you
live—good, clean lives. Girls, keep yourselves virtuous
and worthy of a fine young man who has likewise kept
himself clean, so that together you can go to the house of
the Lord to be sealed in the holy bonds of matrimony for
time and all eternity, and prepare a home where God will
be pleased to send his spirit children. Then you will be
able to face your children secure in the knowledge that
your own example is the way to happiness and eternal
progression. They are entitled to this heritage; I humbly
pray that you will so live as to give it to them.

The whole purpose of the creation of the earth was to
provide a dwelling place where the spirit children of God
might come and be clothed in mortal bodies and, by
keeping their second estate, prepare themselves for salvation and exaltation. The whole purpose of the mission of

Jesus Christ was to make possible the immortality and eternal life of man. The whole purpose of mothers and fathers should be to live worthy of this blessing and to assist God the Father and his Son Jesus Christ in their work. No greater honor could be given to woman than to assist in this divine plan, and I wish to say without equivocation that a woman will find greater satisfaction and joy and make a greater contribution to mankind by being a wise and worthy mother raising good children than she could make in any other vocation.

The Lord has promised us great blessings if we will do our part in this divine plan. President Herbert Hoover gave this incentive: "If we could have but one generation of properly born, trained, educated and healthy children, a thousand other problems of government would vanish. We would assure ourselves of healthier minds, more vigorous bodies, to direct the energies of our nation to greater heights of achievement." (Quoted by President David O. McKay, *Conference Report*, April 1931, pp. 79-80.)

How fortunate we are to have the Church of Jesus Christ established in these latter days, with a prophet of God upon the earth to receive divine revelation and direction for the children of men! We are blessed to know the personality of God, his attributes, and his characteristics. We have been given the plan of life and salvation. We are continually directed as to how we should live so we may have happiness here and eternal life hereafter. We have organizations set up to instruct and educate us in all matters pertaining to our temporal and spiritual welfare.

One of the finest programs the Church has instituted is the family home evening, where all members of the family are called together once a week. It is quite thrilling to me when I contemplate that each Monday evening all over the Church throughout the world our families are gathered together in their homes, and the father, where possible, as head of the house, is directing his family in a discussion of problems pertaining to their spiritual and temporal welfare, using a manual that has been carefully prepared and distributed to each family in the Church. Where these gatherings are held regularly and properly, they are of inestimable value to the family unit, as is evidenced by the many testimonies we receive. I wish to urge every family to follow this program, and I can promise you that as you do so you will be greatly blessed in unity, love, and devotion, and will be delighted with the outcome. Of course, family prayer should be a significant part of this evening, as well as regular family and individual prayer every day.

I can think of nothing sweeter than a home where a man is living his religion and magnifying his priesthood, with his wife supporting him in every way; where love and harmony exist; and where together they are trying to rear a family of righteous sons and daughters whom they can take back into the presence of their Heavenly Father. This may sound like an impossible dream, but I assure you that there are thousands of such families within the Church, and it is something that can be a reality for every one of us as we accept and live the teachings of Jesus Christ. How fortunate a child is to live in such a home, and how great will be the joy of the parents in their posterity!

I repeat: Satan is trying to keep us from the full enjoyment that comes from keeping the commandments of God. We must never forget, and we must teach our children to know, that Satan is real and determined to destroy us. He knows the importance and significance of the family unit. He knows that entire civilizations have survived or disappeared depending on whether the family life was strong or weak. We can keep him out of our homes by living and teaching our children to live the principles of the gospel of Jesus Christ, thereby resisting temptation when it comes, as it surely will.

Girls, prepare yourselves to assume the roles of mothers by gaining knowledge and wisdom through a good education. We teach that the glory of God is intelligence, and so we must all be aware of what is going on around us and be prepared to thwart Satan in his attempts to divert us from our divine destiny. With knowledge, wisdom, determination, and the Spirit of the Lord to help us we can succeed.

We also believe that women should involve themselves in community affairs and in the auxiliary organizations of the Church, but always remember that home and children come first and must not be neglected. Children must be made to feel that mother loves them and is keenly interested in their welfare and everything they do. This cannot be turned over to someone else. Many experiments have been made and studies carried out that prove beyond doubt that a child who enjoys mother's love and care progresses in every way much more rapidly than one who is left in institutions or with others where mother's love is not available or expressed.

Fathers, too, must assume their proper role and responsibility. Children need both parents. Fathers should assume with mothers the duties attendant upon the young children, the discipline and training of the older ones, and be a listening ear for those who need to discuss their problems or want guidance and counseling. Through love, establish a good relationship and line of communication with your children.

I would urge all husbands, fathers, sons, and brothers to show great respect and love and try to be worthy of the women who are our wives, mothers, daughters, sisters, and sweethearts. There is no surer way for a man to show his lack of character, of good breeding, and of quality than for him to show lack of respect for woman or to do anything that would discredit or degrade her. It is unchristianlike, unfair, and displeasing to God for any husband or father to assume the role of dictator and adopt the attitude that he is superior in any way to his wife.

At an area conference in Munich, Germany, President

Harold B. Lee said: "If you husbands remember that the most important of the Lord's work you will ever do will be within the walls of your own home, you can maintain close family ties. . . . If you will strengthen your family ties and be mindful of your children, be sure that home is made a strong place in which children can come for the anchor they need in this day of trouble and turmoil, then love will abound and your joy will be increased."

As women realize the importance of the home and family, and with their husbands keep the commandments of God to multiply and replenish the earth, to love the Lord and their neighbors as themselves, and to teach their children to pray and to walk uprightly before him, then their joy will be increased and their blessings will be multiplied to the extent that they will hardly be able to contain them.

These blessings will be joy and rejoicing in our posterity of healthy, happy children, which blessings those who reject this way of life will never know. There will be peace and satisfaction in the accomplishments of children who succeed and who, in turn, make their own contribution toward making this a better world for generations yet unborn. What a joyous privilege and blessing it will be for those families who, through obedience and love, have prepared themselves to go back into the presence of our Heavenly Father and have it said of each of them: "Well done, thou good and faithful servant . . . enter thou into the joy of thy lord." (Matthew 25:21.)

WOMAN AS MOTHER

Elder David B. Haight

Certain experiences can be recalled vividly throughout our lives. My father was my ideal; then came that unexpected day when as a nine-year-old boy I stood before the open casket of my father. Our brokenhearted mother spoke to us of her love and of how much Father would be missed, but she promised us that we would carry on. We leaned heavily on the faith and understanding of a courageous woman during that crucial time and during the years that followed. We drew on her courage and strength. With limited resources she shepherded us through the challenging years of our youth.

Mother was wise to always keep a cow. A family cow teaches a young boy responsibility, as it requires attention early in the morning and in the early evening. Milk had to be delivered to the neighbor. Mother lovingly but surely guided me through Primary, priesthood preparation, the excitement of Scouting, and even into early dating. Her children came first in her life, and we received through her a continually growing understanding of God's plan and our place in it. Just as vividly as the untimely death of my father, I still feel the loving influence of my mother.

The intervening years have seen many new concepts about a woman's role, but the essentials really have never changed, for they are rooted in eternal principles. A woman's basic role, whereby she fulfills the measure of her creation, is that of motherhood. If we are to clearly understand a woman's role as mother, we need to understand her place in God's eternal design.

The stewardships assigned to man and woman are part of God's eternal plan to prepare us for godhood, and we cannot disregard them without risking our positions in that plan. Adam received his responsibility to be father of the human race and to wrest from the earth that which was needed for his family's temporal existence. Eve also received her responsibility: to bring sons and daughters into this world, to be "the mother of all living." (Moses 4:26.) From the beginning woman was to stand by man's side, sharing with him the divinely bestowed honor, blessings, and responsibilities of governing that which the Lord entrusted to their care. The most precious treasures entrusted to them would be the children whom their Father would send.

Since the dawn of creation no aspect of woman's life compares with her divine appointment to be the vessel for the physical birth of a child who has been nurtured within her. The role of mother is actually made up of countless smaller roles that, throughout the course of her days, she must assume. Mother is a very versatile individual. She is a trusted confidant who may also call us to repent, a builder of character who also repairs broken toys, a healer of wounds who relies as much on kisses as on medicines, a chauffeur who may be delayed until she finishes mending our clothes, an economist who lovingly and skillfully prepares what she buys, a homemaker who teaches the most enduring spiritual lessons, a teacher who enjoys play periods along with her child, a friend who is also our most dedicated servant.

More than any other individual, she occupies the center position in her child's existence. Mother is usually the first person a child sees in the morning and the last to tuck him in at night. She is the one who tenderly kisses away the hurt or cheerfully encourages him on to success.

It is mother who creates an atmosphere of love and contentment in the home. She helps build spirituality in the home. Her attitudes become those of her children. Home is not just a building—it is a spirit and an attitude. Home needs to be a place where the child feels protected and sheltered from the cares of the world, where he can go to be reassured and loved. Mother, through her many virtues, can make of a house a *home.*

Patience is one of those virtues. It is being pleasant when she feels otherwise. It is helping a youngster with school work when she could be relaxing at the end of a busy day. It is helping a child write a letter when she knows it will take much of her precious time for him to say all he has on his mind. It is looking for material for a Sunday School talk when she has her own lesson to prepare. It is keeping her voice calm and sweet when she feels neither calm nor sweet. Patience is doing many things every day that let her family know that they are the center of her life.

The absence of patience leads to one of the most serious problems that plagues our society—child abuse. It is bad enough when an adult takes advantage of a child's vulnerability to inflict mental intimidation, but we now hear and read of those who inflict pain and even some forms of inhuman punishment on sweet and innocent children so recently come from our Father in heaven. He will not tolerate such inhuman behavior. The Lord has warned, "But whoso shall offend one of these little ones . . . it were better for him that a millstone were hanged about his neck, and that he were drowned in the depth of the sea." (Matthew 18:6.)

Unselfishness is synonymous with motherhood. A loving mother truly learns to live for others. She may give up something she wants or would like for the home because of the needs of another member of the family. When a mother exhibits these qualities of patience and unselfishness before her children and does it as though it was a privilege, she has said more to her children of her love for them than she ever could with words.

In large measure a mother's most vital and significant role is as an instructor and trainer. She has the significant hand in molding our Father's precious children, and her influence may be felt not only in this life, but also throughout the eternities.

A child's earliest intellectual stimulation takes place in the home. Mother's gentle encouragement will open the door to the world of knowledge. She not only provides the beginning instruction in such basics as grammar, counting, the alphabet, and even reading and writing, but beyond this she must also stimulate the child's curiosity so his entire life will be enlivened by the search for knowledge and truth.

Reading can be one of the most rewarding experiences that a mother can share with her child. All children love stories, and they love even more a few moments of mother's attention. By reading aloud good stories that reveal worthwhile attitudes and values, she can begin her child on a lifelong adventure that will stretch him far beyond the simple tales that enthrall his mind. She can begin with stories from the scriptures and our Church books. And she mustn't overlook good poetry and a variety of real-life stories and even some make-believe. As her children become conversant with the best that our culture has written, they will become less susceptible to the lure of falsehoods that they will eventually encounter. The youth who loves to read and study will find preparation for his mission and life not a chore, but one more precious jewel on an endless string.

It is at the side of mother that a child learns many important things. It is there that he learns the love of nature and an appreciation for those things which are beautiful. It is at her side and under her tutelage that he learns the social graces.

With the help of a loving and wise mother a child learns dignity and self-respect, as she provides him with the opportunity to work and to share responsibility with other members of the family.

It is mother who takes the time to encourage her son or daughter to pursue a course of study or a noble dream, or to develop a talent. When I was learning to play the violin, my mother insisted that I continue practicing so I could enjoy that which I had started. While the other boys were outside playing ball, I worked at my violin exercises until I had finished my practice period. Sometimes I thought my mother terribly unfair and at times even mean, but with the experience of years and the satisfaction of accomplishment, I now recognize her great love and wisdom.

Our Heavenly Father has given mothers the responsibility not only for bringing children to the earth, but also for preparing them to return to him. As our children so frequently remind us, "Lead me, guide me, walk beside me, /Help me find the way. /Teach me all that I must do/To live with Him some day." ("I Am a Child of God," *Sing With Me,* B-76.)

It is the charge of mother to take these spirit children of our Heavenly Father and give them mortal bodies, and then to love, teach, and guide them back to him. He has trusted his choicest possessions to her care and keeping. He has shown a great deal of love and faith in her. As a loving parent himself, he understands the struggles and achievements, the sorrows and joys. He will never leave us alone. He wants his children to return to him, and he will extend as much help as is needed and will be accepted. The mother who prays frequently and fervently for herself and teaches her children to pray gains access to an unlimited reservoir of wisdom and strength. She remembers not only to pray often, but also to listen to the answers and act upon the promptings he sends.

Effective motherhood is virtually impossible without time of sufficient quantity and quality. President Kimball tells the following story:

"At a distant conference, my plane brought me to the city many hours early. The stake president met me at the airport and took me to his home. Having important work to do, he excused himself and returned to his work. With the freedom of the house, I spread my papers on the kitchen table and began my work. His wife was upstairs sewing. In mid-afternoon, there came an abrupt entry through the front door and a little fellow came running in, surprised to see me. We became friends; then he ran through the rooms calling, 'Mother.' She answered from upstairs, 'What is it, darling?' and his answer was, 'Oh, nothing.' He went out to play.

"A little later another boy came in the front door calling, 'Mother, Mother.' He put his school books on the table and explored the house until the reassuring answer came from upstairs again, 'Here I am, darling,' and the second one was satisfied and said, 'Okay,' and went to play. Another half hour and the door opened again and a young teenager moved in, dropped her books, and called, 'Mother.' And the answer from upstairs, 'Yes, darling,' seemed to satisfy and the young girl began practicing her music lesson.

"Still another voice later called, 'Mother,' as she unloaded her high school books. And again the sweet answer from upstairs, 'I am up here sewing, darling,' seemed to reassure her. She tripped up the stairs to tell her mother the happenings of the day. Home! Mother! Security! Just to know Mother was home. All was well." (*Faith Precedes the Miracle,* Deseret Book, 1972, pp. 117-18.)

These children were not left to themselves. This mother was there to provide and reinforce the security of her children. When mother is needed, she is needed right now, not in a couple hours, or a few minutes. Those children who are left to their own entertainment after school, who come home to an empty house, are more likely to go elsewhere to find someone who will listen to them. Sometimes they are lucky and find someone who can direct them wisely, but more often they find a peer who knows little more than they, or less. Can we take that risk?

Elder Richard L. Evans said: "There are many important things to take the time of mothers these days. But earnestly, urgently, we would say to young mothers: Take time to be there when you are needed, when you are wanted. Take time for open arms; take time for talking and for counsel and correction; take time for sitting down with them, for reading, for singing, for family prayer, for home evenings and hours. Take time with the children for the making of memories, for fixing sure foundations that will last long after less essential things are forgotten." (From *Within These Walls,* New York: Harper and Brothers, 1959, p. 228.)

As the Lord said, "My sheep hear my voice" (John 10:27), so do the little ones respond to their own mothers. Others may clothe and feed and diaper the child, but no one can take the place of mother. This is reinforced by the story of the six-year-old who got lost in a grocery store. He began to call "Martha, Martha." When the mother was found she said: "Honey, you should not call me Martha, I am 'Mother' to you." To which the child responded, "Yes, I know, but the store was full of mothers, and I wanted mine." He didn't want a substitute.

In the parable of the talents the Savior gave us the key when he declared: "Thou hast been faithful over a few things, I will make thee ruler over many things." (Matthew 25:21.) The end of our Father's plan is for us to become gods and goddesses. He helps us toward that goal by giving us responsibilities in the limitations of time that enable us to do on a small scale that which he does on an immense scale in the eternities.

Thus, when a mother honors and magnifies her calling, she is preparing for the eternities. She is not only preparing her children for their eternal destiny, but she is also preparing herself to become a queen and a priestess forever.

As the First Presidency have declared: "Motherhood is near to divinity. It is the highest, holiest service to be assumed by mankind. It places her who honors its holy calling and service next to the angels." (*Conference Report,* October 1942, pp. 12-13.)

May those who are mothers recognize the responsibilities and the opportunities of this divine calling and magnify it. May those of us who are not mothers recognize the sacred, godlike service that women give on our behalf, and may we honor and support them in it.

WOMAN AS A TEACHER

Elder Rex D. Pinegar

"Glory to women! They weave and entwine / Heavenly roses into an earthly life." (Schiller.)

It was my own dear mother, described by some who know her best as the nearest thing on earth to an angel, who was my first teacher. It was she who taught me of my worth as a child of God. It was she who, through her quiet goodness, taught me faith in a living God and in my fellowmen. The indomitable spirit of my wife's mother, through difficult and trying moments, has taught me courage and determination. Her Danish sense of humor and her tireless capacity for work have been inherent qualities that have added strength to our family. My life has been blessed and enriched by five lovely daughters whose love for me and whose expectations of me help me strive harder to be the father and the man they believe in. One of my deepest desires is to become worthy of their confidence and trust. And my beloved wife, Bonnie, provides the crowning touch to my life. She has taught me patience, order, selflessness, and many other important principles.

Each of these special women—and many others with whom I have been associated through the years—does indeed weave and entwine heavenly roses into my earthly life.

I believe the greatest teaching role of woman is that of mother. My wife has been my most influential teacher as she has been a teacher and exemplar to our children. She has reinforced the example of my own mother and enlarged my understanding of the truths I learned as a child. As she has willingly borne our six beautiful children, I have come to a deeper appreciation for all mothers and particularly for my own mother.

21

Using her body as the primal home for her unborn child, the woman teaches us the true example of total sacrifice through the care she takes with herself and the unborn child; her preparations in the home in joyful anticipation of its arrival; her months of discomfort and anxiety; her fulfilling daily responsibilities to her family and to others without complaint; her serenity in waiting; and her glorious expectations. It is from her own mother's love and example that a daughter receives the desire, the hope, the courage, to become herself a mother.

Although it is true that not all women are mothers, each of us was born of a mother and is therefore the benefactor of a mother's love and teachings. And while it may be the lot of some persons to be denied a mother's love and/or teachings following birth, all who are born into this life may know that a woman risked her life to bring them into this wonderful and necessary sphere called mortality.

It has been said that love is the handmaiden of education. The demonstration of this principle through a woman's personal sacrifices should help teach each son or daughter to realize more fully the reality of the love of God and the motivating power of a mother's love.

Psychologists say our first teacher is our physical environment. A child learns what his environment teaches. Though there are innumerable kinds of environments, in a significant way it is the woman who creates the particular environment into which we are born. It is she who teaches us how to interact with our environment in a manner that can bring us happiness and growth. Because the natural physical environment does not allow for the differences in her children, the mother interacts with it and with each child to bring about a positive experience. Women have the seemingly innate ability to turn the harshness of our earthly existence into a world filled with softness, beauty and tenderness. It is this influence upon our environment that brings evidence of heaven to earth.

In their book *Give Your Child a Superior Mind,* authors Siegfried and Therese Engelmann describe the importance of the right kind of environment in a child's learning process, and the contribution a mother makes in creating that type of environment. "She will influence his attitudes and capacity to learn more than any other person in the world, whether she teaches formal subjects or not. She will paint his emotions and help focus his eyes on what is 'important.' She is his most logical teacher." (P. 95.)

It is those informal teachings taught by example and love that mold a child's character and develop his sense of values and self-worth.

President Jimmy Carter, in an address in the Salt Lake Tabernacle on November 27, 1978, emphasized the tremendously important influence his home surroundings had on his life: "My first church was my family," he stated. "I first heard the Bible read in my family. I first heard prayer in my family. I learned about God within my family. My first school was my family; my first government was my family. There in an embryonic stage of growth, I began to perceive the world around me. And when I had questions, they were answered; when I had doubts they were resolved; when I had needs, they were met."

The natural and simple demonstrations of love from a mother to her newborn child—holding, rocking, caressing, and caring for it—create pleasant experiences and secure surroundings for the child to grow and be nurtured in. That environment of love and acceptance is the major source of motivation for the child as his mother's influence and teaching efforts help him build a favorable image toward himself and his ability to do and to achieve. Through her love and encouragement, he may become what perhaps only his mother may believe he can become.

A young man leaving home to serve as a missionary credited his mother for preparing him to accept this challenging assignment. Many times she had reminded him, "Remember, son, average is as close to the bottom as it is to the top. You can be better than average." He believed this because his mother had told him it was so—and he became a better-than-average young man.

In the Book of Mormon, we read the moving story of the young men whom Helaman called "my sons." These two thousand young men demonstrated courage, faith in the Lord, and devotion to his teachings, and they credited their accomplishments to the teachings of their mothers: "Now they never had fought, yet they did not fear death; and they did think more upon the liberty of their fathers than they did upon their lives; yea, they had been taught by their mothers, that if they did not doubt, God would deliver them. And they rehearsed unto me the words of their mothers, saying: We do not doubt our mothers knew it." (Alma 56:47-48.)

President David O. McKay taught that a mother's "ever directing and restraining influence implanted during the first years of his childhood lingers with him and permeates his thoughts and memory as distinctively as perfume clings to each particular flower." (*Gospel Ideals,* p. 452.)

It was said of the great general of the Confederate Army, Robert E. Lee, ". . . that if he was early trained in the way he should go, his mother trained him. If he was 'always good' as his father wrote of him, she labored to keep him so. If his principles were sound and his life a success, to her, more than any other, should the praise be given." The general's brother wrote: "As Robert grew in years, he grew in grace; he was like the young tree whose roots, firmly imbedded in the earth, hold it straight from the hour it was first planted till it develops into majestic proportions. With the fostering care of such a mother, the son must go straight, for she had planted him in the soil of truth, morality, and religion so that his boyhood was marked by everything that produces nobility of character in manhood. The handsome boy was studious and sedate, was popular with other boys, stood high in the estimation of his teachers, and his early inspiration was good, for his first thoughts were directed upon subjects by an excellent mother." (As quoted in Ralston B. Lattimore, ed., *The Story of Robert E. Lee,* Philadelphia: Eastern National Park and Monument Association.)

Someone once said that we are the sum total of all we have experienced. Herein, I feel, is the uniqueness of a woman's contribution in our lives. Her interest and ability in cultivating beauty, grace, culture, and refinement into our lives add immeasurably to the finished product we are striving to become.

My wife began early to borrow recordings of musical masterpieces from the public library to play for our children almost from their birth. One of our earliest purchases following graduate school was a piano. Although she has not formally taught them music, all of our children have acquired a love and appreciation for music of all kinds because she has made music an important part of their environment and has made their formal training in music possible. Music from the piano and the singing voices of children are often heard in our home. Music has been composed, poetry has been written, works of art have been created, and other types of creativity have originated and developed in such an atmosphere.

A mother teaches by example as well as by precept. The modesty of dress of children reflects their mother's example of good taste in dress. Orderliness in their rooms, their organization and use of time, their manners, and their use of good grammar are all tied to their mother's example and expectation of excellence.

Her integrity with them and with her friends and her associates teaches them the principles of brotherhood and respect for all mankind. Her compassion for the downtrodden and her willingness to do for others before doing for herself teaches them the attitude of service.

From my own experience as a father, it has become

apparent to me that those things I desire to have taught to our children are best learned by them when my wife and I are one in purpose and intent. Then her constant presence in the home and her consistent follow-through as circumstances provide the teaching moment bring the most effective and long-lasting learning. I have learned that some of the most effective teaching this father does is through the efforts of his children's mother.

For approximately thirty-seven years my own mother reared her family of ten children with minimum help from an alcoholic husband. Her faith during the long years of disappointment and heartache was finally rewarded with twenty years of faithful devotion of the man she had supported, loved, and kept confidence in. She continually admonished her children to have faith in their father. She promised us that if we honored and respected him, he would someday honor and respect the Lord. Her promise was fulfilled. Her faith has set a pattern for my faith. The effect for good of her example upon her children and her associates has been immeasurable.

Mother's example taught us the meaning and demonstrated the fruits of enduring to the end. She bore testimony of faith daily as she met each challenge with complete confidence in the Lord. It was not easy to do, but her willing heart and her devotion to the Lord and her loyalty to my father were a constant source of strength to the children.

At times we would come in from school or from working in the garden, or caring for the animals, and find traces of tears on Mother's face, but no words of complaint or discouragement ever came from her lips. Through all this we learned the importance of a positive, cheerful attitude, of the value of honest, hard labor. We were taught to do our duty willingly and without complaint. We gained understanding of unconditional love. Her faith in the Lord and her confidence in Dad taught us all the value of love for one another.

As a wife, a woman fills another of her key teaching functions. It is my feeling that many accomplishments a man makes are the result of teachings received from his wife. From the determining of his diet to the development of his attitude toward life, a husband interacts with his wife. A man will usually strive to become everything the woman he loves desires him to be.

In my own life it is not difficult for me to see that the example, counsel, love, and expectations of my wife, Bonnie, have lifted me to a higher, more excellent level of performance of my duties. She has helped me set higher goals and more acceptable objectives for my life than would have been possible had I been left on my own. Always her desire has been to have me do my best. Several times I might have been satisfied with doing less, but her encouragement and expectations have provided the necessary stimulus to search a little deeper for spiritual strength to accomplish the task in a more excellent way.

As our family served in the mission field, it was Bonnie's ability to sense the needs of the missionaries that kept me alert to situations that were more easily attended to because they were recognized at the right time. On one occasion I was faced with a particularly challenging problem. Almost daily, for many months, one of our young missionaries had informed me he was going home. Through persuasion, prayer, faith, and encouragement from myself and others, he had remained in the mission field. On this morning, however, he called to tell me that he had packed his belongings and was definitely on his way home. Nothing I said could change his mind. The only thing I was able to do was to extract a promise from him that he would come to the mission headquarters first. Feeling disappointed and defeated, I went to my wife, Bonnie, to discuss the situation. I frankly admitted that I had tried everything I knew to do. This seemed final. Since he was so determined to leave, I would just have to let him go. Her response was a jarring one. "Oh no you don't!" she exclaimed. "You've held onto this young man for twenty months, and you're not going to give up on him now!" It was true that he had only four months left before he would complete his missionary service. I couldn't give up now, nor could I let him give up!

After agreeing to try again, we prayed for help and guidance. How happy I am to now say that he completed his mission honorably and even served the last three months as a district leader. This inspired woman, my wife, had taught me the importance of persisting, of reaching, of succeeding.

Whenever a task seems too difficult or a seemingly unreasonable request is made of her, Bonnie teaches our family how to meet the challenge successfully. "Would I do it for the Lord?" she asks. The answer can only be "Yes!" Thus we have been taught to accept the challenges of life's experiences as opportunities to prove ourselves faithful to the Lord.

Many are the sacrifices of wives and mothers. Usually a man and woman begin marriage with few of the comforts of life. The husband may be in school or training, confident that the future holds the promise of more and better things with which he will eventually bless his family. Because he is the provider, he is personally involved in the actual labor of acquisition. The wife, on the other hand, finds her contribution to be one of encouragement, building confidence, making do with what she has without complaint. The teachings she provides under these circumstances are largely responsible for the attitudes toward life that the children and even the husband develop.

Bonnie struggled through thirteen years of schooling and professional experience with me. During this time she bore six wonderful children, moved several times, went without comforts in our home to provide educational opportunities for our children, and never complained about the hardships.

My travels over the past several years have permitted

me to be a guest in the homes of over two hundred families. Among these families, I have learned of the efforts of wives to provide their children with the blessings of righteous examples for living. I have learned of sacrifices to put husbands through school, to help family businesses get started, to provide educational and cultural opportunities for children, and to do all these things while continuing to fulfill their divine partnership with God and their husbands—bearing children. It is a wife's vision of the future that permits her to teach by example, patience, long-suffering, and willing sacrifice the value of long-term joy over immediate conveniences, and the importance of faith in the Lord, in one's self, and in the ultimate purposes of life.

One summer day, members of the Sunday School general board were invited by David Lawrence McKay to tour his father's family home in Huntsville, Utah. As we went from room to room, Lawrence shared bits of family history associated with the home. Often hardships, deprivation of comforts, and the absence of loved ones who were called to serve missions had been part of his father's life. He told us how his father, David O. McKay, loved to tell of his own father's return from a mission to Scotland. Grandfather McKay had been called as a missionary after he was married and had several children. The family had eagerly awaited his return. When he arrived home after a long absence, his wife and children greeted him with great affection and joy. One of his daughters asked him if he had seen any miracles on his mission. He is reported to have replied, "The greatest miracle I have ever seen is your mother!" She had taken care of the family, operated the farm without debt, and had even added on rooms to the Huntsville home. Her example of courage, sacrifice, and faith has enhanced the lives of all her family, even to the present generation.

Each of us could probably recount endless examples in which women have been the instruments of God to teach us important lessons and truths.

Even in the life of our Savior Jesus Christ, we find the uniqueness of woman as a teacher. God, our Heavenly Father, came down from his exalted station and selected a woman, Mary, to bear his Only Begotten Son. It was she into whose loving care he entrusted the rearing and preparing of this sacred Son. At Mary's bosom he was nurtured. At her knee he was schooled. It is not unreasonable to suppose that it was she who taught him of his divine birth and mission. These words of a song by Kelly Crabb explain well this beautiful concept:

The First Christmas Story*

"And all they that heard it wondered at those things which were told them by the shepherds. But Mary kept all these things, and pondered them in her heart." (Luke 2:18-19.)

When Jesus was little he sat at the knee
Of Mary, his mother, and asked reverently,
"Tell me, dear Mother, of my birthday again,
"Of shepherds, and angels and three wise men."

(Chorus)
Mary told Jesus the first Christmas story,
How angels had come on a night filled with glory.
Rich men and poor men were there at the start,
And Mary had kept all these things in her heart.

Mary spoke softly as if in a prayer.
She told how the angels had led them all there;
How the shepherds came kneeling to see where he lay,
And to worship a king on that first Christmas day.

Jesus would listen how the kings from afar,
Had followed the light of Bethlehem's star,
And the first Christmas presents they had brought to
*   give*
In return for the gift that all men might live.

---

*©Kelly Crabb, 1977. Used by permission of the author.

Jesus grew up, our Savior, our Lord,
But he always remembered the things he'd heard
From Mary, his mother, who was there at the start,
And he kept all these things, deep in his heart.

Woman is a teacher. To her all the sons of men come for the setting of their course in life. From her each soul receives its launching upon the sea of life. Her harbor is ever beckoning as a refuge from every storm. But the greatest strength of both men and women is shown through the teachings their offspring use to carry them forth safely on the oceans of life. An unknown poet has said, "Ships may ride safely in the harbour, but then/ Ships weren't built to remain in the harbour."

I thank God for the noble women who have taught and who will yet teach me through the heavenly roses they weave into my life.

WOMAN'S RESPONSIBILITY TO LEARN

Elder G. Homer Durham

Three contemporary challenges to intelligence stand out in today's world. The first is the "identity crisis": people, individuals, who do not know who they are. This crisis breeds confusion, alienation, depression, abandonment of moral standards, and an attitude of "doing one's own thing." The drug culture is an alarming expression of it. The second challenge is the decline and disorganization of the family as the stable foundation of society. The third is the scientific-technological revolution. Horrors can result when individuals who have no solid values for guidance and self-restraint and no stable family base have access, in many cases, to high-powered motor cars, computers, jet air travel, rocketry, machine guns, and atomic science.

In such a world, it is woman's responsibility to learn that she is a daughter of a Heavenly Father, with freedom to choose. She must discover what she may become and what she can do, especially with her unique capacity to conceive, bear, nurture, and teach children; with her special physical, emotional, intellectual, and spiritual nature; and with her ability to teach and influence others throughout life.

Woman is endowed by the Creator with the capacity to wield the most civilizing of influences in society. When this influence becomes that of a Jezebel, a Herodias, or a reckless, wicked Julia, daughter of Julius Caesar, society descends to unspeakable degradation. Accordingly, woman has not only to learn, but also to use wisely that which she learns; she must exemplify and teach well the ultimate and intimate things. The world of knowledge is before her. She must enter it and proceed to the limits of her capacity. But, as with man, she will be well-advised to

32

begin with the foundation, the fundamental things: who she is, what she may become, and her role in transmitting those foundation stones so other lives may be built on a solid foundation. She begins by knowing that she is a child of God and recognizing what that portends.

President Spencer W. Kimball has written: "It is a great blessing to be a woman in the Church today. The opposition against righteousness has never been greater, but the opportunities for fulfilling our highest potential have also never been greater."

President Kimball then asked a significant question: "What is our greatest potential? Is it not to achieve godhood ourselves? And what are the qualities we must develop to achieve such greatness?" He listed the following guides for today's woman in the Church: (1) to gain intelligence, light, and knowledge; (2) to develop leadership; (3) to extend, exemplify, and teach in compassion and love.

Woman's place in the Church, and in the ideal world, has long been outlined by our leaders. Man and woman walk together before the Lord as companions, as loving helpmeets to each other, not as self-seeking competitors. Both are children of our Father in heaven. Women as well as men have the potential of which President Kimball spoke, which, when developed, will bless mankind, beginning with the home and family circle and extending thereafter outward in ever-widening circles. Without woman, there would be no home, no family circle.

The responsibility to learn has greater significance for woman today than ever before. Father Adam and Mother Eve were highly endowed with intelligence. Together they learned much through experience, revelation, and studious labor: "And it came to pass that after I, the Lord God, had driven them out, that Adam began to till the earth, and to have dominion over all the beasts of the field, and to eat his bread by the sweat of his brow, as I the Lord had commanded him. *And Eve, also, his wife, did labor with him.*" (Moses 5:1. Italics added.)

Down through the generations, it has been woman's great responsibility to learn and to assist in transmitting knowledge to succeeding generations. As a consequence of the prayers of Adam and Eve, for example, the Lord blessed them "and a book of remembrance was kept, in the which was recorded, in the language of Adam, . . . and by them their children were taught to read and write, having a language which was pure and undefiled." (Moses 6:5-6.)

Having spent many years in universities, which are financed for discovering and disseminating learning, this writer has often reflected on which educational institutions were the more important. The great universities come readily to mind, sometimes with various rankings: Oxford, Cambridge, Paris, Heidelberg, Harvard, Yale, and so on. I have frequently examined research on the learning process with similar questions in mind. I have concluded that the home and family are by far the most significant educational institutions produced by civilization. This opinion is not to detract from the significance of the research centers, hospitals, and institutes that characterize major universities and colleges. Rather, it is to recognize the influence of home and family on the fundamental attitudes that govern conduct, behavior, productivity, mutual helpfulness, the love of learning, and all the values we prize. If these values are not cultivated in the home and family, including during the prenatal period of offspring, all society suffers. Schools and universities cannot strengthen such values in any general, comparable way.

Some homes, like universities, have more competent, dedicated faculties than others. Universities are generally judged by the learning of their faculties and their competence in stimulating further learning. In the home woman is the most important "faculty member"—taking the world as a whole, and measuring "faculty competence" in terms of the quality and quantity of time spent with the "students."

Child neglect and child abuse are among the greatest evils of the day. Perhaps equally significant, if not as dramatic, are the homes that fail to recognize the true nature and character of human life and of the earth and universe in which we dwell; homes that ignore our dependence upon external forces and especially upon Divine Providence for all that we have and are. The home may be influential in producing a Joseph Smith, a Mary Fielding Smith, a Brigham Young, an Abigail Adams, an Esther, Ruth, or Rebekah, a Beethoven, an Einstein, a Cornelia, a Florence Nightingale, a Madame Curie. A home may also be an influence in producing less agreeable, less admirable, even despicable personalities, some of whom wreak havoc in the lives of peoples and nations largely through ignorance of the fundamental truths.

In addressing an area conference in Paris, France, July 31, 1976, Sister Camilla Kimball, beloved wife of President Spencer W. Kimball, made the following points:

1. The role of mother is the most exacting and difficult of all professions.

2. A woman should, therefore, be skilled in child training, in psychology and sociology, in economics and management, in nutrition and nursing. She should seek a well-rounded education.

3. It is vitally important that a woman cultivate, through study, prayer, and the exercise and example of faith, those great spiritual qualities that produce a rich and valid religious and learning atmosphere not only in the home but also in society.

Speaking in practical terms Sister Kimball said: "I would hope that every girl and woman here has the desire and the ambition to qualify in two vocations—that of homemaking, and that of preparing to earn a living outside the home, if and when the occasion requires. An unmarried woman is always happier if she has a vocation in which she can be socially of service and financially independent." Speaking of married women, Sister Kimball noted that any married woman "may become a widow without warning. Property may vanish as readily as a husband may die. Thus, any woman may be under the necessity of earning her own living and helping to support dependent children." Also emphasized was the fact that the later years of a woman's life "should be viewed as a time that can be socially and professionally productive. . . . The active woman cannot hold her hands. . . ." (*Ensign*, March 1977, pp. 58-59.)

Women who are married, single, or widowed can have tremendous influence in keeping the ship of society stable, tranquil, and truly progressive amid the storms of modern life.

Civilization is based on family, home, and marriage. Although these institutions may exist in various forms and in various cultures, their fundamental importance remains. A graphic and dramatic example of this, and of the interdependence of man and woman, was found in the early culture of the Eskimo. While the woman was dependent upon the man as fisher and hunter for food, fur, clothing, and fuel, the man was utterly dependent upon the woman's learning and skill in producing the warm gloves and the life-preserving inner and outer garments that made the hunt possible in sub-zero Arctic temperatures.

Man, as well as woman, has obligations to learn the difficult art of fatherhood in homemaking. This is not a task just for the woman. However, in altogether too many cases the role of fatherhood is one that is exercised in absentia, with infrequent moments when the father's intelligence and knowledge are applied to the deep concerns of family life. Quality of family time, as well as quantity, is often reduced to the minimum by the busy world of work and other priorities. As recent television and radio announcements sponsored by the Church have stated so effectively, "Give your children everything—give them your time!" Family home evening should be religiously kept as a happy, joyous experience.

No matter how competent the father, the breadth and depth of his knowledge, or his spiritual qualities, the primary influence in the lives of men and women is in the hands of woman. She is at the very heart of civilization. If the great educational institution known as home and family does not function, things turn for the worse. Where family prayer, family devotions, and well-spoken, polite, and courteous language are accompanied by study, learning, compassion, and love, society and civilization flourish. The rise of the Roman Republic can be read in the integrity, the mutual help, and the deep religious faith of the pre-empire Roman family. The decline of the Roman Empire can be starkly read in the history of the decline of the Roman family, of marriage, and of its religious and moral foundations.

President Brigham Young, in the Church's pioneer days, clearly saw the relations of woman's learning in the household arts to the vast field of liberal-professional education. Said he, speaking on the education of daughters, "I would not have them neglect to learn music and would encourage them to read history and the scriptures, to take up a newspaper, geography, and other publications, and make themselves acquainted with the manners and customs of distant kingdoms and nations, with their laws, religion, geographical location on the face of the world, their climate, national productions, the extent of their commerce, and the nature of their political organization; in fine, let our boys and girls be thoroughly instructed in every useful branch of physical and mental education." (*Journal of Discourses* 9:189.)

Modern revelation has told us that "the glory of God is intelligence, or, in other words, light and truth." (D&C 93:36.) As the glory of her Father is intelligence, so is the glory of woman intelligence, or, in other words, light and truth. Light and truth, we are told, "forsake that evil one." (D&C 93:37.) It is important that individual lives, homes, and families be set in order. The responsibility of learning first things first, keeping them foremost, then building thereon, becomes one of woman's great missions. The influence of woman on mature man is as profoundly significant as her influence on children. All human beings are involved in each other's lives. It would appear from scripture, from history, and from observation that women have a capacity to exercise unusual influence for the uplift of culture, character, morals, high ideals, and true religion.

There may be some thoughtful, devoted women, and many others outside the realm of Church membership, who feel that the dual role of homemaking and liberal-vocational-professional education for women places too much emphasis upon the former and not enough upon the latter. To this it may be replied that, in the light of history, it is impossible to overemphasize the importance of what Sister Kimball described as "the most exacting and difficult of all professions," namely that of mother. Sister Kimball knows the learning required of lawyers, surgeons, engineers, architects, chemists; yet she lists motherhood as the most exacting and difficult.

To restrict, hamper, thwart, contain, or stunt the development of woman's education and talents is contrary to the most basic gospel concepts. Such can be read in the accounts of the creation, whether in Genesis or in the Pearl of Great Price. Mormon women have stood among the pioneers of American educational, political, and professional activity since the nineteenth century. Not all may have received the message or found it possible. But the guiding principles are there. Within three months of the organization of the Church, on July 1, 1830, the Lord, in a revelation for the benefit of Emma Smith, revealed that "all those who receive my gospel are sons and daughters in my kingdom." (D&C 25:1.) Emma was further told that she should be "ordained under his [Joseph's] hand to expound scriptures, and to exhort the church, according as it shall be given thee by my Spirit. For he shall lay his hands upon thee, and thou shalt receive the Holy Ghost, and thy time shall be given to writing, and to learning much." (D&C 25:7-8.)

Today, Mormon women are numbered among leading physicians, lawyers, architects, engineers, professors, technicians, artists, writers, teachers, and outstanding homemakers. The record is clear. Woman's responsibility to learn is clear. A man cannot be saved in ignorance, nor can a family, nor a nation. Woman plays the most fundamental, character-building role in helping to combat the forces of ignorance that breed disease, famine, and human misery. Moreover, she can add to her learning her woman's spirit.

A story is told of a pioneer wagon about to descend the famous "Hole-in-the-Rock" defile to the Colorado River. Joseph Stanford Smith had been below helping earlier wagons cross the river. Climbing back up the rugged ascent, he found his own wagon, his wife, Arabella, their baby, and three other children waiting. They had to descend alone, without men and ropes behind to slow their descent of a forty-five-degree grade strewn with boulders. The husband hesitated, saying, "I'm afraid we can't make it." His courageous wife, her small babe wrapped securely in the back of the wagon, replied, "But we've got to make it." She and an old horse held the vehicle from behind. Thrown to the ground, dragged to the bottom of the gorge, her flesh torn, Arabella was undaunted. And thus the wagon made its hazardous descent and crossed the river. (David E. Miller, *Hole-in-the-Rock. An Epic in the Colonization of the American West,* University of Utah Press, 1959, pp. 111-15.)

What one individual woman can do, all can. This has been described well by Dr. Anne G. Osborn, neuroradiologist, a faculty member of the University of Utah College of Medicine. In an article titled "The Ecstasy of the Agony: How to Be Single and Sane at the Same Time," Dr. Osborn disclosed a great secret that shows the importance of learning and doing for all women, single, married, widowed, or divorced. She analyzed the value of time and the wide variety of ways in which time may be put to use; then she recorded: "I have found that a sure cure for depression [one might also say loneliness] is to realize *someone out there needs me.*" (*Ensign*, March 1977, pp. 47-49.)

Here is a significant clue for women throughout time and history. Not only is there "someone out there" who needs you; there are tens, hundreds, thousands. In most cases, what you achieve and what you do as a consequence of what you know and learn can affect a multitude—even the very course of events.

THE ETERNAL COMPANIONSHIP: HUSBAND AND WIFE

Elder LeGrand Richards

Our first record of marriage was when the Lord placed Adam in the Garden of Eden: "And the Lord God said, It is not good that the man should be alone; I will make him an help meet for him." (Genesis 2:18.)

Since it was "not good that the man should be alone" before he became subject to death through transgression, why should man assume it will be good to be alone when he is redeemed from the effects of the fall? If man needed a helpmeet before he was subject to death, he should need a helpmeet when his body is restored, through the resurrection, to its former state.

Let us consider another statement of the Lord: "And they shall be one flesh." (Genesis 2:24.) It is evident that the Lord did not have in mind that they should be one in purpose and desire, for he makes himself clear as to what this oneness should consist of: "one flesh."

Jesus understood this principle fully, as we learn from his statement: "For this cause shall a man leave his father and mother, and cleave to his wife; And they twain shall be one flesh: so then they are no more twain, but one flesh. What therefore God hath joined together, let not man put asunder." (Mark 10:7-9.)

Thus Jesus gave us to understand that both man and wife should be "one flesh." Why should men claim they separate at death if those same bodies of flesh and bone come forth from the grave? The apostle Paul understood this relationship and said: "Nevertheless neither is the man without the woman, neither the woman without the man, in the Lord." (1 Corinthians 11:11.) In other words, so far as the Lord is concerned, man and woman are not "twain, but one flesh."

41

"For this cause shall a man leave his father and mother, and shall be joined unto his wife, and they two shall be one flesh. . . . Nevertheless let every one of you in particular so love his wife even as himself; and the wife see that she reverence her husband." (Ephesians 5:31, 33.)

The apostle Peter understood that the husband and wife would inherit eternal life together and not separately. After referring to Abraham and Sarah, Peter said: "Likewise, ye husbands, dwell with them according to knowledge, giving honour unto the wife, as unto the weaker vessel, and as being heirs together of the grace of life; that your prayers be not hindered." (1 Peter 3:7.)

The prophet Isaiah described conditions as they shall exist upon the earth when the earth is renewed and receives its paradisiacal glory:

"For behold, I create new heavens and a new earth: and the former shall not be remembered, nor come into mind. . . .

"And I will rejoice in Jerusalem, and joy in my people: and the voice of weeping shall be no more heard in her, nor the voice of crying.

"There shall be no more thence an infant of days, nor an old man that hath not filled his days: for the child shall die an hundred years old; but the sinner being an hundred years old shall be accursed.

"And they shall build houses, and inhabit them; and they shall plant vineyards, and eat the fruit of them.

"They shall not build, and another inhabit; they shall not plant, and another eat: for as the days of a tree are the days of my people, and mine elect shall long enjoy the work of their hands.

"They shall not labour in vain, nor bring forth for trouble; for they are the seed of the blessed of the Lord, and their offspring with them.

"And it shall come to pass, that before they call, I will answer; and while they are yet speaking, I will hear.

"The wolf and the lamb shall feed together, and the

lion shall eat straw like the bullock: and dust shall be the serpent's meat. They shall not hurt nor destroy in all my holy mountain, saith the Lord." (Isaiah 65:17, 19-25.)

We gather from Isaiah's prophecy that when the Lord creates a new heaven and a new earth, then shall "the seed of the blessed of the Lord, and their offspring with them," build houses and inhabit them and plant vineyards and eat the fruit therefrom. How can anyone figure out anything other than the organization of family groups? What else can one understand from the statement, "the seed of the blessed of the Lord, and their offspring with them"? Who will occupy houses when built, if not families?

How can righteous men and women who have teamed together in the rearing of their children, and sacrificed for them and for each other, believe that the righteousness or justice of God would put an end to their association and companionship? God will not, if they are married for eternity by the priesthood of God, for they without us cannot be made perfect nor we without them. This is the Lord's plan, and he gave it to his children, for his children; it is divine.

The Lord has also revealed, through the Prophet Joseph Smith, that in the resurrection we will receive our children who have died in infancy, and will have the privilege of rearing them to manhood and womanhood: "And the earth shall be given unto them for an inheritance; and they shall multiply and wax strong, and their children shall grow up without sin unto salvation. For the Lord shall be in their midst, and his glory shall be upon them, and he will be their king and their lawgiver." (D&C 45:58-59.)

This refers to conditions during the millennial reign of the Lord Jesus Christ for a thousand years upon this earth. "And there shall be no sorrow because there is no death. In that day an infant shall not die until he is old; and his life shall be as the age of a tree; And when he dies he shall not sleep, that is to say in the earth, but shall be changed in the twinkling of an eye, and shall be caught up, and his rest shall be glorious." (D&C 101:29-31.)

Thus The Church of Jesus Christ of Latter-day Saints stands alone in teaching the doctrine of the eternal duration of the marriage covenant and family unit. How can anyone in whose heart burns a true love for the wife of his bosom and for his own children do other than want to believe this doctrine? What could eternity offer to interest one unless he could enjoy it with those whom he has loved in mortality and with whom he has spent his life?

At the close of the apostle Paul's wonderful sermon on the resurrection he exclaimed: "O death, where is thy sting? O grave, where is thy victory? The sting of death is sin; and the strength of sin is the law." (1 Corinthians 15:55-56.)

Had Paul not understood that death was but a brief separation from those whom we love and that there would be a reuniting of loved ones in the resurrection, he might well have said, "The sting of death is eternal separation from those we have loved in life." But Paul understood the truth, for he had been caught up into the third heaven and the paradise of God. (See 2 Corinthians 12.)

Regardless of the teachings of their churches to the contrary, there are many who believe they will be united again with their loved ones.

Anderson M. Baten dedicated a poem to his beloved wife, Beulah, entitled "The Philosophy of Life," which expresses his faith that his marriage tie would extend beyond the grave:

> I wed thee forever, not for now;
> Not for the sham of earth's brief years,
> I wed thee for the life beyond the tears,
> Beyond the heart pain and the clouded brow,
> Love knows no grave, and it will guide us, dear,
> When life's spent candles flutter and burn low.

Add the Lord's own words in a revelation to the Prophet Joseph Smith at Nauvoo, Illinois, recorded July 12, 1843, relating to the new and everlasting covenant of marriage:

"Therefore, if a man marry him a wife in the world, and he marry her not by me nor by my word, and he covenant with her so long as he is in the world and she with him, their covenant and marriage are not of force when they are dead, and when they are out of the world; therefore, they are not bound by any law when they are out of the world.

"Therefore, when they are out of the world they neither marry nor are given in marriage; but are appointed angels in heaven, which angels are ministering servants, to minister for those who are worthy of a far more, and an exceeding, and an eternal weight of glory.

"For these angels did not abide my law; therefore, they cannot be enlarged, but remain separately and singly, without exaltation, in their saved condition, to all eternity; and from henceforth are not gods, but are angels of God forever and ever." (D&C 132:15-17.)

Compare the limited promise made to those whose marriage vows are for this world only with the promise contained in the revelation to the Prophet Joseph Smith made to those who covenant in marriage for time and for all eternity: ". . . it shall be done unto them in all things whatsoever my servant hath put upon them, in time, and through all eternity; and shall be of full force when they are out of the world; and they shall pass by the angels, and the gods, which are set there, to their exaltation and glory in all things, as hath been sealed upon their heads, which glory shall be a fulness and a continuation of the seeds forever and ever." (D&C 132:19.)

With this glorious truth revealed anew to men upon this earth, they really have something to live for and something to die for. We doubt if there ever has been a truth revealed to man upon this earth as comforting as the revelation of the Lord to the Prophet Joseph Smith concerning the new and everlasting covenant of marriage.

WOMAN'S RELATIONSHIP TO THE PRIESTHOOD

Elder James M. Paramore

My dear daughter: On the eve of your marriage I want to take this opportunity to tell you how proud we are of you and of your desires to establish a home of your own that will be filled with the power of love, of sacrifice; that will be filled with the laughter of children; and one that may be built upon some fundamental, timeless principles.

As I have seen you grow to maturity and prepare for this day, my heart has been full, for you have always seemed to search out the best—even the highest—and have clung fast to those things which at once bring peace and direction to your life.

Dear one, the Lord foresaw that all mankind should come to this important juncture. He has commanded us to establish our own homes, have children, and learn through our Father's greatest workshop, the home, the lessons that would prepare us best to return to his presence prepared to know and understand his ways. Establishing a home is perhaps the most sacred yet awesome responsibility given to man. In such a home are fostered love, character, learning, sacrifice, selflessness, devotion to one another, to God, and to our country; and such an undertaking is surely the grandest of all of man's work. You, my dear, will be at the center of that important crucible, for your influence will serve all the ends of those within the family and those who will come under the influence of each of its members.

One of the most beautiful descriptions of a wife and mother's influence and work is stated in the thirty-first chapter of Proverbs, verses 10 through 31. I commend this to you for your review as some priceless thoughts of a prophet.

As you look around you, daughter, you will see that the world will not always espouse those things counseled by the Lord. By every standard of rational judgment and evaluation society is undergoing at a reckless, almost unprecedented rate such enormous shifts in long previously-adhered-to values and priorities that the outcomes are frightening. With an increase in the standard of living in the nations of the world, a thrust toward materialism has resulted. Shifts in people's basic value systems are undergoing great structural change, which change is heralded and accepted as timely and symptomatic of a great liberation of man and woman. The value-generating institutions of the family and religion are not only being threatened, but also questioned as to validity and necessity.

Some of the concerns become apparent as one sifts through the voices of the so-called liberated—the magazines, mass media, and even the programs major companies are designing to anticipate and be ahead of the changes in order to capitalize on them. Many of these writers suggest—

Instant gratification, at whatever cost, now or deferred.

A *new work ethic*—a philosophy to "work to live" instead of "live to work." This includes increasing numbers of women working, not out of necessity as may be required to sustain life, but out of a desire to increase one's material acquisitions.

A *new theology of pleasure*, which makes pleasure more important than work.

A *credit explosion* where some reports indicate that as much as 55 percent of the total income of many families is already committed to credit installments.

Altered home life-styles—more affluence, more divorce, a liberation mania that supports personal gratification, less sacrifice, fewer or no children to burden our life-styles, and on and on.

All of these philosophies of the world are being bought with careless abandon in every quarter of the world, and even some of our Church members are being lulled away ever so slowly. It is a day described in the first section of the Doctrine and Covenants in a revelation given to the Prophet Joseph Smith:

". . . and the day cometh that they who will not hear the voice of the Lord, neither the voice of his servants, neither give heed to the words of the prophets and apostles, shall be cut off from among the people;

"For they have strayed from mine ordinances; . . .

"They seek not the Lord to establish his righteousness, but every man walketh in his own way, and after the image of his own God, whose image is in the likeness of the world. . . ." (D&C 1:14-16.)

Against that backdrop, the destiny of the world, of man, of woman, of the home, and of eternity is clearly enunciated by the voice of the Lord and taught by prophets and apostles with authority, with the experience of the generations past, and with revelations from on high to guide man with confidence, security, and high purpose and promise. The majesty of God, his priesthood, and the relationship of man and woman to them are essential for every man and woman on this earth to understand if they are to be secure and guided toward their ultimate destiny.

You see, there is an order to the things of God, and that order is ordained of the Lord to bless you, your husband, and your children throughout all generations of time. Because this is so important to a true order of happiness in your home, I would like to leave just a thought or two about your relationship to your husband, to the priesthood, to your family, and to the philosophies of the world.

Daughter, the Lord has spoken through his prophets on these fundamental principles in the home and our relationships to each other. Think of this advice, which may well be scorned in the world:

"I say to the sisters, seek to have confidence in your husbands, and believe that they are capable of leading you; and when you seek instruction, believe them capable of giving it to you; and be faithful, humble, and obedient to them. Their feelings should not be concentrated in you, but your feelings should be in them, and theirs should be in those who lead them in the Priesthood. Their feelings are concentrated in the Lord their God and what is ahead, and there is where they should be. You should be glad to see them step forward and walk onward in the path of their duty, and not require them to devote themselves to you to the exclusion of things and duties of life which lie before them. As they progress and lead on, you will feel to travel in the same road. This is the order, and if order is maintained in this thing, you will see the beauty of it; and it will be a satisfaction to you and them to believe that your husband, he who is at your head, is progressing in the things of God." (Daniel H. Wells, *Journal of Discourses* 4:256.)

As I think of this counsel of Brother Wells, I remember an experience that occurred a number of years ago. A very capable priesthood leader, who was qualified by years of faithful service to the Church, ably trained in his profession, and astute in working with and motivating people, found himself in a very frustrating situation. Nearly every time he would leave the home to perform his duties in the Church he would be confronted by his wife, who, in essence, forced him to make a decision between the Church or staying with her. There were no unusual health problems or special conditions that required him to be at home every minute—only a possessiveness on her part. This constant reluctance by her to sustain, encourage, and assist her husband in very heavy responsibilities caused him ultimately to have to be released and, more importantly, weakened the family to such a point that all the blessings of that family unit—earthly and heavenly—were placed in jeopardy. The tragic ending was divorce, family members separated, bitterness, increased financial burdens, and so forth.

My dear, can we ignore the counsel of the Lord, who,

through the apostle Paul, said: "For the man is not of the woman; but the woman of the man. Neither was the man created for the woman; but the woman for the man. For this cause ought the woman to have power on her head because of the angels. Nevertheless neither is the man without the woman, neither the woman without the man, in the Lord." (1 Corinthians 11:8-11.)

I believe that from the beginning God has made it manifestly clear that woman has a very special place, a position that is clearly defined and articulated with regard to her destiny in the divine plan. Both man and woman are a part of this plan—neither is without the other. But their roles do differ.

The man is in God by the power of the priesthood; so even is the woman in the man. One—the man, by virtue and power of the priesthood—is to have power over those things delegated to him. That is, he is to exercise his priesthood by organizing his home upon the principles of righteousness. He takes the leadership in these roles; he presides, teaches, trains, and encourages. The priesthood is the authority of God delegated to man to accomplish these worthy purposes (and others), and to assist the Father in training His children to walk through this mortal life and prepare for eternity. The man is to set this in order, to deliberately live worthy and know the will of God concerning this highest of purposes and objectives.

Through the Prophet Joseph Smith the Lord has told us that the revelations have been given from heaven "that every man might speak in the name of God the Lord, even the Savior of the world." Why? "That faith also might increase in the earth; That mine everlasting covenant might be established." (D&C 1:20-22.)

Elder John A. Widtsoe wrote: "By divine fiat, the Priesthood is conferred on the men. This means that organization must prevail in the family, the ultimate unit of the Church. The husband, the Priesthood bearer, presides over the family; the Priesthood conferred upon him is intended for the blessing of the whole family.

Every member shares in the gift bestowed, but under a proper organization. No man who understands the gospel believes that he is greater than his wife, or more beloved of the Lord, because he holds the Priesthood, but rather that he is under the responsibility of speaking and acting for the family in official matters. It is a protection to the woman who, because of her motherhood, is under a large physical and spiritual obligation. Motherhood is an eternal part of the Priesthood." (*Evidences and Reconciliations*, Bookcraft, 1960, pp. 307-8.)

So here we see the roles of man and woman defined by prophets who spoke as moved upon by the Spirit. Man would be crowned with the priesthood—the power to bless his family and others; while woman would be for the man, a helpmeet to accomplish the purposes of God for all His children. Her role would not include receiving the priesthood; rather, it would be a special role, designated by God, to be a co-creator with him to "multiply, and replenish the earth, and . . . bring forth thy children; and thy desire shall be to thy husband, and he shall rule over thee." She would become "the mother of all living." (Genesis 1:28; 3:16, 20.)

These are concepts lost to the world by disobedience and pride. But they are not lost to God, who has enunciated them in all dispensations of time to his prophets. They have stood the test of time, for they are eternal and essential to the ultimate patriarchal order of families where righteous men, under the power of the priesthood of God, will bind their wives and children together for eternity.

Once these principles are understood, we can then begin to see why the roles of family, fatherhood, motherhood, and eternal relationships would come under constant attack by the world and the philosophies of men—all motivated by Satan, who would seek to deceive us to lust after carnal desires.

The priesthood is not assumed by anyone, neither men nor women, but is bestowed on worthy men by those having the authority to bless and build the kingdom of God on earth. Its ultimate purpose is to provide every family with the patriarchal sealing ordinances performed in the temple of God, that every son and daughter of God will take his or her rightful place in this patriarchal order.

The priesthood quorums are the constituted bodies to which all holders of the priesthood belong, and, when properly utilized, will bless the people—every family. "The Priesthood of the Son of God, which we have in our midst, is a perfect order and system of government, and this alone can deliver the human family from all the evils which now afflict its members, and insure them happiness and felicity hereafter." (*Discourses of Brigham Young*, p. 130.)

Daughter, I remember some thoughts that were given to the priesthood members a few years ago to help us see how this all works in a home: "To illustrate how the home and the priesthood tie in together let us suppose that the home is a sort of a quorum—the *patriarchal quorum of the home*. The father is the quorum president; unlike other presiding officers in the Church, no one can release or remove him from office. He is supreme in his family. In his home he presides over all visitors, no matter what their church or state position. His wife is his counselor; his children, the quorum members." ("Melchizedek Priesthood in the Home," *Improvement Era*, April 1958, pp. 250-51.)

Do you remember one of the manuals you recently studied in the Church? The following scripture and thoughts were used to help you understand its very important meaning on this subject of sustaining your husband and the role of a wife. This helps you to see the important relationships that you will need to understand and establish:

"Wives, submit yourselves unto your own husbands, as unto the Lord.

"For the husband is the head of the wife, even as

Christ is the head of the church: and he is the saviour of the body.

"Therefore as the church is subject unto Christ, so let the wives be to their own husbands in every thing.

"Husbands, love your wives, even as Christ also loved the church, and gave himself for it." (Ephesians 5:22-25.)

Remember these thoughts you studied? The main thought was that as Christ is to his church, so the man is to his wife.

This means that:	And also that:
Christ loves the Church.	The husband loves his wife as an extension of himself.
Christ sacrificed himself in behalf of the Church that it might be sanctified.	The husband desires to sanctify his wife and is willing to sacrifice in her behalf.
The Church is obedient to the commands of Christ.	The wife is submissive to the righteous guidance of her husband.

The apostle Paul says "this is a great mystery" (Ephesians 5:32), for the way of man, especially in our day, is to frustrate these truths and confuse our thinking in favor of equal roles, not differentiated roles and purposes. Your great opportunity will be to strengthen your husband and children in everything. You will be a source of infinite comfort, encouragement, wisdom, love, and kindliness to rebuild them as they experience the normal challenges of everyday living. They will feel in you strength and glory and steadfastness, for these are virtues vested in you by a loving Heavenly Father for his explicit purposes. "Neither is the man without the woman," but both sustain the work of the Father and of the home and marriage by these innate and predetermined explicit roles. Each role is dependent upon the other.

Now, daughter, one of the greatest of all heresies today is that while marriage may be acceptable, children are not. Listen to a few quotations from a current author reporting on "The New Minority":

"The model is no longer the family. Now it is of two young people, both working, who can afford a lifestyle that historically only the very rich could enjoy. Children have lost their place in our society. As a society we really don't like children. Now, the husband and wife typically put their own interests first, their joint goals second and any family interests beyond the couple third.

"Between 1973 and 1976 the number of sterilizations among married couples leaped 25 percent. Now increasing numbers of people want no children—period. Child rearing is one of the biggest casualties of the modern age that is being ushered in by this generation." (David Johnston, "The New Minority," *Sundancer*, September 1978.)

These philosophies are born out of man's own vain thinking, which in the end leaves him precious little. They may even be subscribed to by some of our own people who don't understand the need for spiritual children to come to earth and take bodies and experience and overcome the world. How does this philosophy stack up against the counsel the Lord has given to "be fruitful, and multiply, and replenish the earth"?

Subsequent prophets have said that the purpose of marriage is to provide opportunity for our Father's spiritual children to come to earth to take on bodies and be tested. They have counseled that the family is the schoolmaster where both parents and children learn sacrifice, learn how to love, learn how to sustain each other through life's challenges, and prepare for eternity.

Can the world ignore these commands from the prophets with impunity? No! A resounding "no" to that question. How else will sacrifice and love be acquired and inculcated into the heart of man? But God's law shall not be frustrated, for his laws are eternal and irrevocable because they are true.

You ask, what if there are no children or if a girl is

not permitted to marry—what about them? Again we look to the prophets for answers, and Brigham Young gave this advice:

"Many of the sisters grieve because they are not blessed with offspring. You will see the time when you will have millions of children around you. If you are faithful to your covenants you will be mothers of nations . . . and when you have assisted in peopling one earth, there are millions of earths still in the course of creation. And when they have endured a thousand million times longer than this earth, it is only as it were the beginning of your creations. Be faithful, and if you are not blest with children in this time, you will be hereafter." (*Journal of Discourses* 8:208.)

We all know of some who have lost their husbands while there are still children in their homes. What of this, you ask? I remember one morning listening to a woman who had just lost her husband while still rearing six small children. I shall remember her because of the spirit that she possessed. She expressed to the group assembled her great gratitude to the Lord for the wonderful, faithful, priesthood-bearing husband she had been privileged to have for ten years. She told how beautiful and wonderful it was for her and her children to have lived under his authority and direction those years and how privileged she was to have been selected to give up her husband for a greater call of the Lord. What an honor it was for her to be sealed to that great man, and her joy was complete in knowing she was sealed to him for eternity. The Spirit bore witness to me then of God's great love for his children, for earth life is but a day in the passage of eternity, and to have known God, his majesty and infinite love, and to have had one's eternity sealed up with a righteous man is surely one of the greatest gifts of God.

Forgive me, dear, for sending such a long letter, but your roles to the priesthood and as wife and mother are so important to the Lord and to your mother and me that

I wanted you to hear and feel my deepest thoughts and concerns. Remember, as someone once said, the Church is not on casters to be moved about by the will of man. The principles we have discussed today have been taught and reiterated since the beginning of the world. Listen to this thought of President Stephen L Richards, a former member of the First Presidency: "They [the women of the Church] know that that priesthood has true virtue within it—the power to bless, the power to heal, the power to counsel, to make peace and harmony prevail." (*Conference Report,* April 1958, p. 95.)

Dear daughter, this great power can, if properly exercised by the husband and father, bless the wife, the mother, and the children. Remember to love, sustain, obey, be a helpmeet, counsel, guide, and nurture. Parents are really the first "home teachers" established by the Lord to protect and surround the family as a refuge against the world—a refuge that, when administered under the influence of the priesthood, is the only sure defense.

Yes, as President Spencer W. Kimball has said, the home is the place to save society—and you, dear, are at the center of that sacred, eternal, and patriarchal institution.

Sincerely,
Your devoted
father

EVE AND THE FALL

Elder Bruce R. McConkie

The three most important
things to occur in all eternity; the three things that
transcend in importance anything that has ever occurred
in the infinite past or will ever occur in the endless future; the three things without which either all things
would vanish away, or the whole purpose of existence
would come to naught—these three, an eternal trinity of
superlatives, are as follows:

1. The creation of all things by God the Father,
assisted by Jehovah, Michael, and others.

2. The fall of man, as accomplished by Adam and
Eve.

3. The atonement of Christ, which was made possible
because the Son of God had an immortal Father and a
mortal mother.

These three, the crowning events of the eternities, are
united as one. They are inseparably intertwined. The fall
of man was made possible because of the nature and kind
of creation that rolled forth by the hand and word of the
Almighty; and the atonement of Christ, through which
salvation comes, is built on the foundation of Adam's
fall.

God our Heavenly Father is the Creator, Upholder,
and Preserver of all things. By his Only Begotten he made
the worlds, the sidereal heavens, the universe, and all
things that in them are. As we shall see, he made this
temporal planet as a home for Adam and Eve and all His
worthy spirit children. And he created it in an immortal
or paradisiacal state and placed on it two immortal per-
sonages whose bodies were made from the dust of the
earth, so that through their acts the earth would become
a mortal sphere and thus a fit abode for mortal men.

Adam and Eve were placed in the Garden of Eden to carry out the purposes of the Eternal Father—to introduce mortality to this earth, and to begin the process of providing mortal bodies for the spirit children of their Eternal Father.

The Lord Jesus Christ came in the meridian of time to ransom men from the effects of the fall—to reclaim them temporally and spiritually.

Thus if there had been no creation, there could have been no fall, no temporal and spiritual death, no mortal probation, no course that prepares the offspring of God to become like him and to reign with him in immortal glory forever.

And if there had been no fall of man—no change in his constitution; no temporal death, which is the separation of body and spirit; no spiritual death, which is death as pertaining to the things of righteousness and of the Spirit—there could have been no atoning sacrifice, no redemption, no deliverance, no resurrected immortality, and no eternal life or exaltation in the kingdom of God.

We have thus singled out the three most transcendent events of all eternity—the creation, the fall, and the atonement—and have mentioned the intertwined relationship that binds them together, so that as we consider the fall of man (the fall of Adam and the fall of Eve) we may have all things in their proper perspective and relationship to each other.

Now let us consider the position of Eve in this eternal scheme of things.

1. Eve Before Eden.

Who was Adam and who was Eve when they twain dwelt in the presence of the Father in that premortal life before the foundations of this earth were laid?

They were spirit children of the Father. Adam, a male spirit, then called Michael, stood next in power, might, and dominion to the Lord Jehovah. Eve, a female spirit, whose premortal name has not been revealed, was of like stature, capacity, and intelligence.

Christ and Adam were companions and partners in preexistence. Christ, beloved and chosen of the Father, was foreordained to be the Savior of the world; Adam, as the great Michael, led the armies of heaven when Lucifer and one-third of the spirit hosts rebelled. The Lord Jesus, then reigning as the Lord Jehovah, was the number one Spirit Son; described as being "like unto God" (Abraham 3:24), he then ascended the throne of eternal power; and with him, by his side and serving under his direction, was Michael, who is Adam, and who was then foreordained to be the first man and the head of the human race.

And we cannot doubt that the greatest of all female spirits was the one then chosen and foreordained to be "the mother of the Son of God, after the manner of the flesh." (1 Nephi 11:18.) Nor can we do other than suppose that Eve was by her side, rejoicing in her own foreordination to be the first woman, the mother of men, the consort, companion, and friend of mighty Michael.

Christ and Mary, Adam and Eve, Abraham and Sarah, and a host of mighty men and equally glorious women comprised that group of "the noble and great ones," to whom the Lord Jesus said: "*We* will go down, for there is space there, and *we* will take of these materials, and *we* will make an earth whereon these may dwell." (Abraham 3:22-24. Italics added.) This we know: Christ, under the Father, is the Creator; Michael, his companion and associate, presided over much of the creative work; and with them, as Abraham saw, were many of the noble and great ones. Can we do other than conclude that Mary and Eve and Sarah and myriads of our faithful sisters were numbered among them? Certainly these sisters labored as diligently then, and fought as valiantly in the war in heaven, as did the brethren, even as they in like manner stand firm today, in mortality, in the cause of truth and righteousness.

2. Eve in Eden.

From the Celestial Presence to a garden planted eastward in Eden; from life as a spirit in the presence of

59

God to life on this earth in a tabernacle of clay; from the realms of eternal light to the dark recesses of life on planet earth—this was one giant step forward for Adam and Eve. By first obtaining bodies made of the dust of the earth, our first parents commenced the course whereby they could obtain resurrected bodies like those of other exalted beings, including the exalted Father of us all.

How did Adam and Eve gain their temporal bodies? Our revelations record Deity's words in this way: "And I, God, said unto mine Only Begotten, which was with me from the beginning: Let us make man in our image, after our likeness." (Moses 2:26.) Man on earth—Adam and Eve and all their descendants—was to be created in the image of God; he was to be in his image spiritually and temporally, with power to convert the image into a reality by becoming like him. Then the scripture says: "And I, God, created man in mine own image, in the image of mine Only Begotten created I him; male and female created I them." (Moses 2:27.) Also: "And I, the Lord God, formed men from the dust of the ground, and breathed into his nostrils the breath of life; and man became a living soul, the first flesh upon the earth, the first man also." (Moses 3:7.)

For those whose limited spiritual understanding precludes a recitation of all the facts, the revealed account, in figurative language, speaks of Eve being created from Adam's rib. (Moses 3:21-25.) A more express scripture, however, speaks of "*Adam*, who was *the son of God*, with whom God, himself, conversed." (Moses 6:22. Italics added.) In a formal doctrinal pronouncement, the First Presidency of the Church (Joseph F. Smith, John R. Winder, and Anthon H. Lund) said that "all who have inhabited the earth since Adam have taken bodies and become souls in like manner," and that the first of our race began life as the human germ or embryo that becomes a man. (See *Improvement Era*, November 1909, p. 80.)

Christ is universally attested in the scriptures to be

the Only Begotten. At this point, as we consider the "creation" of Adam, and lest there be any misunderstanding, we must remember that Adam was created in immortality, but that Christ came to earth as a mortal; thus our Lord is the Only Begotten in the flesh, meaning into this mortal sphere of existence. Adam came to earth to dwell in immortality until the fall changed his status to that of mortality.

Those who have ears to hear will understand these things. All of us, however, must know and believe that when Adam and Eve were placed in the Garden of Eden, there was no death. They were immortal. Unless some change occurred they would live forever, retaining all the bloom, beauty, and freshness of youth. Joseph Smith, Brigham Young, Orson Pratt, and our early brethren preached many sermons on this.

Also, though they had been commanded to multiply and fill the earth with posterity, Adam and Eve, in their then immortal state, could not have children. Nor could they be subject to the tests, trials, and probationary experiences of mortality. Hence, came the need—the imperative, absolute need—for the fall, for the change in status that would bring children, death, and testing into the world.

3. The Fall of Adam and Eve.

As to the imperative need imposed upon our first parents to undergo that change of status which bears the name "the fall of Adam" or "fall of man," and as to the rationale that underlies it, I have written elsewhere:

To "the first man of all men" (Moses 1:34), who is called Adam, and to "the first of all women," who is Eve, "the mother of all living" (Moses 4:26)—while they were yet immortal and thus incapable of providing mortal bodies for the spirit children of the Father—the command came: "Be fruitful, and multiply, and replenish the earth." (Moses 2:28.)

Be fruitful! Multiply! Have children! The whole plan of salvation, including both immortality and eternal life for all the spirit hosts of heaven, hung on their compliance with this command. If they obeyed, the Lord's purposes would prevail.

If they disobeyed, they would remain childless and innocent in their paradisiacal Eden, and the spirit hosts would remain in their celestial heaven—denied the experiences of mortality, denied a resurrection, denied a hope of eternal life, denied the privilege to advance and progress and become like their Eternal Father. That is to say, the whole plan of salvation would have been frustrated, and the purposes of God in begetting spirit children and in creating this earth as their habitat would have come to naught.

"Be fruitful, and multiply." 'Provide bodies for my spirit progeny.' Thus saith thy God. Eternity hangs in the balance. The plans of Deity are at the crossroads. There is only one course to follow: the course of conformity and obedience. Adam, who is Michael—the spirit next in intelligence, power, dominion, and righteousness to the great Jehovah himself—Adam, our father, and Eve, our mother, must obey. They must fall. They must become mortal. Death must enter the world. There is no other way. They must fall that man may be.

Such is the reality. Such is the rationale. Such is the divine will. Fall thou must, O mighty Michael. Fall? Yes, plunge down from thy immortal state of peace, perfection, and glory to a lower existence; leave the presence of thy God in the garden and enter the lone and dreary world; step forth from the garden to the wilderness; leave the flowers and fruits that grow spontaneously and begin the battle with thorns, thistles, briars, and noxious weeds; subject thyself to famine and pestilence; suffer with disease; know pain and sorrow; face death on every hand—but with it all bear children; provide bodies for all those who served with thee when thou led the hosts of heaven in casting out Lucifer, our common enemy.

Yes, Adam, fall; fall for thine own good; fall for the good of all mankind; fall that man may be; bring death into the world; do that which will cause an atonement to be made, with all the infinite and eternal blessings which flow therefrom.

And so Adam fell as fall he must. But he fell by breaking a lesser law—an infinitely lesser law—so that he too, having thereby transgressed, would become subject to sin and need a Redeemer and be privileged to work out his own salvation, even as would be the case with all those upon whom the effects of his fall would come. (*The Promised Messiah,* Deseret Book, 1978, pp. 220-21.)

4. The Man Adam and the Woman Eve.

When we speak of the fall of Adam, do we have reference to the man Adam as an individual? Or to Adam as a generic term for the human race? Or to the term *Adam* as meaning both the man Adam and the woman Eve? When we speak of the fall of man are we talking about the fall of a male individual? Or of man in the generic sense that includes women as part of mankind? What of the woman Eve and her fall?

God, meaning the Father, created Adam and Eve in his own image; male and female created he them. (Moses 2:27.) The woman was given to the man in eternal marriage, for there was no death. They were commanded not to partake of the tree of the knowledge of good and evil. But "when the woman saw that the tree was good for food, and that it became pleasant to the eyes, and a tree to be desired to make her wise," as the figurative language has it, "she took of the fruit thereof, and did eat, and also gave unto her husband with her, and he did eat. And the eyes of them both were opened." (Moses 4:12-13.)

It is of this event that Paul says: "And Adam was not deceived, but the woman being deceived was in the transgression." (1 Timothy 2:14.) Thus we read of the transgression of Eve. Our revelations also say: "The devil tempted Adam, and he partook of the forbidden fruit and transgressed the commandment." (D&C 29:40.) Indeed, many scriptures speak of "Adam's transgression" (Romans 5:14), though we are left to conclude that Eve fell first and then Adam, speaking of these two as individuals.

Our understanding of the fall comes into true focus when we ponder these words from the book of the generations of Adam: "In the day that God created man, in the likeness of God made he him; In the image of his own body, male and female, created he them, and blessed them, and called *their* name Adam, in the day when *they* were created and became living souls in the land upon the footstool of God." (Moses 6:8-9. Italics added.)

Thus the name of Adam and Eve as a united partnership is Adam. They, the two of them together, are named Adam. This is more than the man Adam as a son of God or the woman Eve as a daughter of the same Holy Being. Adam and Eve taken together are named Adam, and the fall of Adam is the fall of them both, for they are one.

5. Eve After Eden.

We are led to believe that the name Adam means *first father* and reason therefrom that the name Eve means *first mother*. We know that Adam was the first man of all men and that Eve is "the mother of all living." (Moses 4:26.)

Lehi says, "If Adam had not transgressed he would not have fallen, but he would have remained in the garden of Eden." Then he adds: "And they"—meaning Adam and Eve—"would have had no children." Hence the epigrammatic conclusion: "Adam fell that men might be." (2 Nephi 2:22-25.)

Thus it was that "Adam knew his wife, and she bare unto him sons and daughters, and they began to multiply and to replenish the earth. And from that time forth, the sons and daughters of Adam began to divide two and two in the land, and to till the land, and to tend flocks, and they also begat sons and daughters." (Moses 5:2-3.) Eden was behind them and the earth before them. The purposes of the Lord were underway.

While Adam and Eve were yet in Eden, the Lord "gave unto them"—meaning the revelation came to *both* of them—"commandments that they should love and serve him, the only living and true God, and that he should be the only being whom they should worship." (D&C 20:19.) Then came the fall.

After the fall "Adam and Eve, his wife, called upon

the name of the Lord, and they heard the voice of the Lord . . . speaking unto them . . . and he gave unto them commandments, that they should worship the Lord their God," including the offering of sacrifices. Be it noted that both the man and the woman prayed; both heard the voice of the Lord; and both were commanded to worship him.

Then Adam offered sacrifices, an angel appeared and bore record of Christ, the Holy Ghost fell upon Adam, and Adam prophesied many things. "And Eve, his wife, heard all these things and was glad, saying: Were it not for our transgression we never should have had seed, and never should have known good and evil, and the joy of our redemption, and the eternal life which God giveth unto all the obedient." Then Adam and Eve "blessed the name of God," taught the gospel to their children, and continued in prayer and devotion. (Moses 5:4-12.)

Again, be it noted that the Lord is not dealing with Adam alone. Both of the eternal partners are glorying in the wonders of the gospel and walking in the light of heaven. Eve is a full partner; she is a helpmeet to her husband in both temporal and spiritual things.

6. Eve in the Eternal Eden.

In a not distant day this "earth will be renewed and receive its paradisiacal glory." (Article of Faith 10.) The Edenic, paradisiacal state that covered the face of the whole earth in a primeval day will be restored, and the millennial era will be ushered in as the Lord Jesus returns in all the glory of his Father's kingdom.

Before that day Adam, who is the Ancient of Days, will preside at a great conference to which all those of every dispensation who have held keys and positions of presidency on earth will come. The appointed place for this assemblage is Spring Hill, Daviess County, Missouri, which is named by the Lord "Adam-ondi-Ahman, because, said he, it is the place where Adam shall come to visit his people, or the Ancient of Days shall sit, as spoken of by Daniel the prophet." (D&C 116.)

Daniel's testimony is: "I beheld till the thrones were cast down, and the Ancient of days did sit, whose garment was white as snow, and the hair of his head like the pure wool: his throne was like the fiery flame, and his wheels as burning fire.

"A fiery stream issued and came forth from before him: thousand thousands ministered unto him, and ten thousand times ten thousand stood before him: the judgment was set, and the books were opened. . . .

"I saw in the night visions, and, behold, one like the Son of man came with the clouds of heaven, and came to the Ancient of days, and they brought him near before him.

"And there was given him dominion, and glory, and a kingdom, that all people, nations, and languages, should serve him: his dominion is an everlasting dominion, which shall not pass away, and his kingdom that which shall not be destroyed." (Daniel 7:9-10, 13-14.)

That is to say, after all to whom the keys of God's earthly kingdom have been given have reported their stewardships to Adam, after Adam has received back again the keys delegated to his descendants, then Christ will come, take them unto himself, and reign personally on earth for the space of a thousand years. This is a great initial day of judgment at which Adam presides.

Now what of Eve? Will she and the sisters play a part in this and other great events that lie ahead? The scriptures are silent on the point. We are left to formulate an answer that accords with the great and eternal principles that have been revealed. We know, to some extent, the part she played—at Adam's side—in the past. We cannot believe that she is other than by his side now, or that she will depart therefrom in future days.

In our hymnbook we have the song "Sons of Michael, He Approaches," in which we raise our voices in glad acclaim to Adam and sing of what he will do at Adam-ondi-Ahman. One of the verses is a paean of praise to Eve.

Mother of our generations,
Glorious by great Michael's side,
Take thy children's adoration;
Endless with thy Lord preside;
Lo, lo, to greet thee now advance,
Thousands in the glorious dance!

This of course, assumes that she and other faithful women will continue to stand and serve at the sides of their husbands in the glorious events ahead.

Speaking of the eternal state of exaltation and of those who then live in the married state, the Lord says: "Then shall *they* be gods, because *they* have no end; therefore shall *they* be from everlasting to everlasting, because *they* continue; then shall *they* be above all, because all things are subject unto *them*. Then shall *they* be gods, because *they* have all power, and the angels are subject unto *them*." (D&C 132:20. Italics added.)

What shall we say, then, of Eve—as an individual and as a generic name for all women who believe and obey as she did? Would we go far astray if we came up with such conclusions as the following?

Eve—a daughter of God, one of the spirit offspring of the Almighty Elohim—was among the noble and great in preexistence. She ranked in spiritual stature, in faith and devotion, in conformity to eternal law with Michael, who participated in the creation of the earth and who led the hosts of heaven when Lucifer and his rebels were cast out.

As she was at Michael's side before the foundations of the earth, so she came with him into Eden. The two of them there performed for all men the inestimably great service called the fall of man. Thus, mortality, the begetting of children, the probations of this life, and the hope of eternal life and exaltation—all these become available to all of the children of the Father of us all.

After the fall, Eve continued to receive revelation, to see visions, to walk in the spirit. As Adam became the pattern for all his sons, so did Eve for all her daughters. And as they twain have gone on to exaltation and sit upon their thrones in glorious immortality, so may all, both male and female, who walk as they walked.

As there are no words to extol the greatness of the Ancient of Days unto whom thousands of thousands shall minister and before whom "ten thousand times ten thousand" shall stand in a day of judgment, so there is no language that can do credit to our glorious mother Eve.

Let God be praised for the glorious plan of creation, redemption, and exaltation. And let Adam and Eve be praised for the infinitely great part they have played in the eternal plan of the Eternal One.

TO THE ELECT
WOMEN OF THE
KINGDOM OF GOD

President Ezra Taft Benson

In the Doctrine and Cov-
enants the Lord designates Sister Emma Smith "an elect
lady." (D&C 25:3.) To you faithful sisters of the Church,
I address you as the Elect Women of the Kingdom of
God. Commenting on the phrase "an elect lady," the
Prophet Joseph Smith said that elect means "to be elected
to a certain work." (HC 4:552.) I call you "elect women,"
for you have been elected by God to perform a unique
and sacred work in our Heavenly Father's eternal plan.

In the beginning, God placed a woman in a companion role with the priesthood. The Gods counseled
and said that "it was not good that the man should be
alone; wherefore, I will make an help meet for him."
(Moses 3:18.) Why was it not good for man to be alone?
If it were only man's loneliness with which God was
concerned, he might have provided other companionship.
But he provided woman, for she was to be man's
helpmeet. She was to act in partnership with him.

In this pronouncement that it was not good for man
to be alone, God declared a fundamental truth. The Lord
God gave woman a different personality and tempera-
ment than man. By nature woman is charitable and bene-
volent, man is striving and competitive. Man is at his best
when complemented by a good woman's natural
influence. She tempers the home and marriage relationship with her compassionate and loving influence.

Yes, it is not good for man to be alone because a
righteous woman complements what may be lacking in a
man's natural personality and disposition. Nowhere is
this complementary association more ideally portrayed
than in the eternal marriage of our first parents, Adam
and Eve.

The scriptures tell us that "Adam began to till the earth . . . as . . . the Lord had commanded him. And Eve, also, his wife, did labor with him . . . and they began to multiply and to replenish the earth. . . .

"And Adam and Eve blessed the name of God, and they made all things known unto their sons and their daughters. . . . And Adam and Eve, his wife, ceased not to call upon God." (Moses 5:1-2, 4, 12, 16.)

From this inspired record we see that Adam and Eve provide us with an ideal example of a covenant marriage relationship. They labored together; they had children together; they prayed together; and they taught their children the gospel—together. This is the pattern God would have all righteous men and women imitate.

In the world today, there are observed strenuous efforts to distort and desecrate this divine pattern. We hear much talk—even among some of our own sisters—about so-called "alternative life-styles" for women. It is maintained that some women are better suited for careers than for marriage and motherhood, or that a combination of both family and career is not inimical to either. Some have even been so bold as to suggest that the Church move away from the "Mormon woman stereotype" of homemaking and rearing children. God grant that that dangerous philosophy will never take root among our Latter-day Saint women!

I repeat: You are elect *because* you were elected to a certain work. How glorious is the knowledge that you are dignified by the God of heaven to be wives and mothers in Zion!

The Church recognizes that not all women in the Church will have the opportunity for marriage and motherhood in mortality. Of necessity, some of our sisters have had to choose careers as a means of their own livelihood, and in some instances to provide for their families. But we do not encourage our young women to enter careers as lifelong objectives nor as alternatives to marriage and family. There is a godly and noble reason for this counsel. You were not created to be the same as men. Your natural attributes, affections, and personalities are entirely different from those of a man. They consist of faithfulness, benevolence, kindness, and charity. They give you the personality of a woman. They also balance the more aggressive and competitive nature of a man.

The business world is competitive and sometimes ruthless. We do not doubt that women have both the brainpower and the skills—and in some instances superior abilities—to compete with men. But by competing they must, of necessity, become aggressive and competitive. Thus their godly attributes are diminished and they acquire a quality of sameness with man.

Recently I received a letter from a sister who has spent most of her life in the work force, providing a second income to the home. Her marriage finally ended in divorce. Her greatest concern was that she felt robbed by not having the time to teach her own children the lasting spiritual values, a woman's godly prerogative.

The conventional wisdom of the day would have you be equal with men. We say, we would not have you descend to that level. More often than not the demand for equality means the destruction of the inspired arrangement that God has decreed for man, woman, and the family. Equality should not be confused with equivalence. It is well to remember the inspired counsel of President David O. McKay: "Woe to that home where the mother abandons her holy mission or neglects the divine instruction, influence, and example—while she bows, a devotee at the shrine of social pleasure; or neglects the essential duties of her own household, in her enthusiasm to promote public reform." (*Conference Report*, October 1907, p. 63.)

When the Relief Society was organized by the Prophet Joseph Smith, he said, "The Church was never perfectly organized until the women were . . . organized." ("The Story of the Organization of the Relief Society," *Relief Society Magazine*, March 1919, p. 129.) The Prophet gave the women of the Church this inspired counsel, which is as appropriate today as when it was given. Listen to how a woman is to use her attributes and nature to complement man:

"This is a charitable Society, and according to your natures; it is natural for females to have feelings of charity and benevolence. You are now placed in a situation in which you can act according to those sympathies which God has planted in your bosoms. . . .

". . . You need not be teazing your husbands because of their deeds, but let the weight of your innocence, kindness and affection be felt, which is more mighty than a millstone hung about the neck; not war, not jangle, not contradiction, or dispute, but meekness, love, purity—these are the things that should magnify you in the eyes of all good men. . . .

"If this Society listens to the counsel of the Almighty, through the heads of the Church, they shall have power to command queens in their midst. . . .

". . . Let this Society teach women how to behave towards their husbands, to treat them with mildness and affection. When a man is borne down with trouble, when he is perplexed with care and difficulty, if he can meet a smile instead of an argument or a murmur—if he can meet with mildness, it will calm down his soul and soothe his feelings; when the mind is going to despair, it needs a solace of affection and kindness. . . .

"When you go home, never give a cross or unkind word to your husbands, but let kindness, charity and love crown your works henceforward; don't envy the finery and fleeting show of sinners, for they are in a miserable situation; but as far as you can, have mercy on them, for in a short time God will destroy them, if they will not repent and turn unto him.

"Let your labors be mostly confined to those around you, in the circle of your own acquaintance, as far as knowledge is concerned, it may extend to all the world; but your administering should be confined to the circle of your immediate acquaintance, and more especially to the members of the Relief Society." (HC 4:605-7.)

One apparent impact of the women's movement has been the feelings of discontent it has created among young women who have chosen the role of wife and mother. They are often made to feel that there are more exciting and self-fulfilling roles for women than housework, diaper changing, and children calling for mother. This view loses sight of the eternal perspective that God elected women to the noble role of mother and that exaltation is eternal fatherhood and eternal motherhood.

Many years ago, a mother successfully reared her nineteen children to adulthood. She did so almost totally without her husband's help because he, a minister, was imprisoned because of his religious beliefs. Later, one of her sons wrote to her and inquired how she was able to accomplish the marvelous feat of successfully rearing her large family. She modestly replied: ". . . The writing anything about my way of education I am much adverse to. It cannot, I think, be of service to anyone to know how I, who have lived such a retired life for so many years, used to employ my time and care in bringing up my own children. No one can, without renouncing the world, in the most literal sense, observe my methods; and there are few, if any, that would entirely *devote above twenty years of the prime of life in hopes to save the souls of their children,* which they think may be saved without so much ado; for that was my principal intention, however unskillfully and unsuccessfully managed." (Franklin Wilder, *Immortal Mother,* New York: Vantage Press, 1966, p. 43.)

That mother was Susannah Wesley, and the son who wrote was John Wesley, founder of the Methodist Church and one of the great Reformers. Twenty years of the prime of life in the hopes of saving the souls of her children! Such a task requires skill, competence, intelligence, and ingenuity far above any career, and in the eternal perspective is the essence of glorious fulfillment.

When Susannah Wesley informed her husband that

she was teaching the nineteen children Bible lessons in what must have been the first Sunday School, her husband wrote back and mildly rebuked her. She replied with that intuitive inspiration with which God graces women who do their elected work: "I reply that as I am a woman, so am I a mistress of a large family. And though the superior charge of the souls contained in it lies upon you, as head of the family, and as their minister, yet in your absence I cannot but look upon every soul you leave under my care as a talent committed to me under a trust, by the great Lord of all the families of Heaven and earth. And if I am unfaithful to Him, or to you, in neglecting to improve these talents, how shall I answer unto Him when He shall command me to render an account of my stewardship?" (Ibid., p. 108.)

There, in the powerful words of a Christian mother, is the eternal perspective of a woman who understood her noble role and the work God had elected her to do.

Today, I pay grateful tribute to two elect women who have influenced my life—my mother and my own sweetheart and eternal companion. I thank God that they have used their womanly attributes of compassion and charity to bless my life and the lives of all their posterity. I bless them that their posterity will hold them in remembrance and love forever.

Mother was Relief Society president in her ward, a small but solid country ward. I remember how important father considered her work in that assignment. Father gave to me, as the oldest of seven at that time and of eleven later, the responsibility of harnessing the horse and getting the buggy ready for mother's two-o'clock weekly Relief Society meetings. This had to be done by one o'clock so she could be there early. At that time I was not tall enough to buckle the collar or put the bridle on the horse without getting on the fence or a box. In addition, I was to take half a bushel of wheat from our granary and put it in the back of the buggy. In those days the Relief Society sisters were building up a storage of wheat against a time of need. Following World War I the United States government called for that wheat to relieve hunger in Europe.

When mother was called to visit the sick in the ward or to help mothers with new babies, it was always by horse and buggy. As the buggy rolled down the dirt road, the circling wheels left a track that stayed even after the buggy disappeared. Mother's influence has also stayed—in my life and in the countless lives she blessed through compassionate service and example. How well she followed the admonition of the Prophet Joseph Smith to "let your labors be mostly confined to those around you, in the circle of your own acquaintance . . . and more especially to the members of the Relief Society."

And to my own eternal companion: there are few things in the world that give a man such courage as the faith of a noble companion who says, more effectively in her actions than in her words, "I will be happy with what you can provide, and I have faith that you will, with my help, provide for our needs."

Often a woman shapes the career of her husband, or brother, or son. A man succeeds and reaps the honors of public applause when, in truth, a steadfast and courageous woman has in large measure made it all possible; has, by her tact and encouragement, held him to his best; has had faith in him when his own faith has languished; has cheered him with the unfailing assurance, "You can, you must, you will."

May I acknowledge how greatly my wife's loving devotion, inspiration, faith, and loyal support have contributed to whatever success may be ours. Since the happy day she became my bride, and we left for Iowa in an old battered Ford, I have never heard a murmur from her lips. She has never given me a single worry except when she was ill, and that has been, with but few exceptions, only with the responsibilities of motherhood.

Under all conditions and circumstances she has been the perfect lady. Her rich heritage and education have enabled her to be a true helpmeet; her congeniality, fine sense of humor, and interest in my work have made her a pleasing companion; and her unbounded patience and intelligent insight into childhood have made her a most devoted mother. These and other virtues, combined with her loyalty and self-sacrificing devotion to her husband, impel me to crown her the sweetest, most helpful, most inspiring sweetheart and wife that ever inspired a man to noble endeavors.

To all you sisters—elect women of God—may he bless you to ever keep before you your unique and sacred honor. May he bless you with increased qualities of faithfulness, benevolence, kindness, and charity that you may always complement your husbands and the priesthood of God.

THE BLESSINGS AND RESPONSIBILITIES OF WOMANHOOD

President Spencer W. Kimball

Although the organizational details of the Church's programs for women may change from time to time, the basic program is always the same. We call upon all women to gear their lives and train their children as in the past, only more so. We give to you the admonition of the great apostle Paul as he spoke to the Ephesian converts:

"Finally, my brethren [and that means sisters too], be strong in the Lord, and in the power of his might.

"Put on the whole armour of God, that ye may be able to stand against the wiles of the devil.

"For we wrestle not against flesh and blood, but against principalities, against powers, against the rulers of the darkness of this world, against spiritual wickedness in high places." (Ephesians 6:10-12.)

Our women are among the best educated and best trained. We encourage all of you to keep abreast of the times, to be familiar with current events, to be able to read the signs of the times, to be prepared to direct your children in the proper paths to guarantee to them a purposeful and eventful life. Paul says to put on the whole armor of God. All of you who are students of the scriptures know of Satan, the father of lies. You know how he turns the truth into a lie. He garnishes evil to make it appear beautiful, pleasing, easy, and even good. He told the prophet Moses, "Worship me." Moses was alert enough to ask, "Where is thy glory? Who art thou?" Moses had already gone through an experience with his Lord, who had told him, "No man can behold all my glory, and afterwards remain in the flesh on the earth."

Moses had been given a great vision by God, who had protected him so that he could see and hear and not be consumed. He beheld God with his spiritual eyes. Moses said that he would have withered and died in the bright presence of the Lord but for the Lord's protection.

Then, in questioning Satan, Moses said, "I could not look upon God except he strengthen me with his glory, but you Satan, where is your glory? For I can look upon you with my natural eyes. God said unto me, Worship God, for him only shalt thou serve."

Moses again said, "I will not cease to call upon God." Satan then resorted to his last chance. He said, "I am the Only Begotten, worship me." In his great fear, Moses said again, "Depart from me, Satan, for this one God only will I worship. In the name of the Only Begotten, depart hence, Satan." (See Moses 1:1-24.)

That is a good statement to be used by every soul who is besieged by this father of lies.

When he is challenged, Satan is angry, as he was with Moses. He cried with a loud voice, trembled, and shook, and he departed from Moses, who was resolute. There was weeping and wailing and gnashing of teeth as he departed from Moses. There was nothing else for him to do. He has to leave when we say, "Depart from me, Satan." Every soul who has mortality is stronger than Satan, if that soul is determined.

Temptations are great. Satan tells us that black is white. He lies to us; therefore, we must be prepared to make a bold stand before him, for he is without flesh and blood, and against principalities and powers and the rulers of darkness. We need the whole armor of God that we may withstand. We must quench the fiery darts of the wicked with the shield of faith.

As you sisters read the papers, watch television, hear the radio, and read books and magazines, much that comes to your consciousness is designed to lead you astray. Much of what you read may be scurrilous. But you are intelligent. You have learned from your infancy what is right. You know what you want for your children. You must make your own decisions in determining if it is right or wrong.

Some of those who write for the public have already gone after that which is far afield. They have chosen already to subvert the right way. They are telling you that it is not necessary to marry; it is not necessary to marry to have children; it is not necessary to have children; you may have all the worldly pleasures without these obligations and responsibilities. There is the pill. There is abortion. There are other ways to give you this loosely held, so-called freedom. They are telling you that you are manacled to your homes, to your husbands, to your children, to your housework. They are talking and writing to you about a freedom they know nothing about.

Only she is free who knows no master, either Satan or his emissaries. Our only master should be the Savior. It was the apostle Paul who said, "To whom ye yield yourselves to obey, his servants ye are to whom ye obey." (Romans 6:16.)

The Lord said: "And ye shall know the truth, and the truth shall make you free."

The Jews to whom he was speaking answered him, "We be Abraham's seed, and were never in bondage to any man: how sayest thou, Ye shall be made free?

"Jesus answered them, Verily, verily, I say unto you, Whosoever committeth sin is the servant of sin. . . .

"If the Son therefore shall make you free, ye shall be free indeed. . . .

"Ye are of your father the devil, and the lusts of your father ye will do. He was a murderer from the beginning, and abode not in the truth, because there is no truth in him. [He is still a murderer; he will always be a murderer.] When he speaketh a lie, he speaketh of his own; for he is a liar, and the father of it.

"And because I tell you the truth, ye believe me not." (John 8:32-34, 36, 44-45.)

The role of woman was fixed even before she was

created, and God is the same yesterday, today, and forever. It is written: "And I, God, created man in mine own image, in the image of mine Only Begotten created I him; male and female created I them. [The story of the rib, of course, is figurative.] And I, God, blessed them [man here is always in the plural; it was plural from the beginning] and said unto them: Be fruitful, and multiply, and replenish the earth, and subdue it, and have dominion over it." (Moses 2:27-28.)

What a beautiful partnership! Adam and Eve were married for eternity by the Lord. Such a marriage extends beyond the grave. All peoples should call for this kind of marriage.

"And Adam knew Eve his wife; and she conceived, and bare Cain, and said, I have gotten a man from the Lord." (Genesis 4:1.)

"This is the book of the generations of Adam. In the day that God created man, in the likeness of God made he him; Male and female created he them; and blessed them, and called their name Adam, in the day when they were created." (Genesis 5:1-2.)

This is a partnership. And as God completed this magnificent creation, he looked it over and pronounced it "very good" (Genesis 1:31)—something that isn't to be improved upon by our modern intellectuals: the male to till the ground, support the family, and give proper leadership; the woman to cooperate, bear the children, and rear and teach them. It was "very good."

And that's the way the Lord organized it. It wasn't an experiment. He knew what he was doing. Those things that endanger a happy marriage are infidelity, slothfulness, selfishness, abortion, unwarranted birth control, leaving the home to others, and sin in all of its many manifestations.

Eve, so recently from the eternal throne, seemed to understand the way of life, for she was happy that she and Adam had eaten the forbidden fruit. Adam blessed God and began to prophesy because his eyes were opened; he realized that in this life there should be joy for them, and that in the course of events they should again see God in the flesh. Eve also was glad; she said, "Otherwise we never would have had children." (Moses 5:11.) She, like other normal women, wanted children. She and Adam both rejoiced in their confirmed status. Nephi wrote, "All things have been done in the wisdom of him who knoweth all things." There were no guesses here, no trial and error. "Adam fell that men might be; and men are, that they might have joy." (2 Nephi 2:24-25.)

So our beloved mother Eve began the human race with gladness, wanting children, glad for the joy that they would bring to her, willing to assume the problems connected with a family, but also the joys.

Since infancy we have been singing the beloved song "O My Father," its meaning only partly understood by many people. Sister Eliza R. Snow gave us these words and I think they are magnificent. In every funeral of the Kimball family as long as I can remember, "O My Father" was the principal song.

> O my Father, thou that dwellest
>   In the high and glorious place,
> When shall I regain thy presence,
>   And again behold thy face?
> In thy holy habitation,
>   Did my spirit once reside?
> In my first primeval childhood,
>   Was I nurtured near thy side?
>
> For a wise and glorious purpose
>   Thou hast placed me here on earth,
> And withheld the recollection
>   Of my former friends and birth.
> Yet oft-times a secret something
>   Whispered, "You're a stranger here;"
> And I felt that I had wandered
>   From a more exalted sphere.

I had learned to call thee Father,
Through thy Spirit from on high,
But until the key of knowledge
Was restored, I knew not why.
In the heavens are parents single?
No; the thought makes reason stare!
Truth is reason, truth eternal
Tells me I've a mother there.

When I leave this frail existence,
When I lay this mortal by,
Father, Mother, may I meet you
In your royal courts on high?
Then, at length, when I've completed
All you sent me forth to do,
With your mutual approbation
Let me come and dwell with you.
—Hymns, no. 138

Man became a living soul—mankind, male and female. The Creators breathed into their nostrils the breath of life, and man and woman became living souls. We don't know exactly how their coming into this world happened, and when we're able to understand it the Lord will tell us.

As an indication of the importance the Gods gave to women, the Lord said, "Therefore shall a man leave his father and his mother, and shall cleave unto his wife: and they shall be one flesh." (Genesis 2:24.)

Do you note that? She, his wife, occupies the first place. She is preeminent, even above the parents who are so dear to all of us. Even the children must take their proper but significant place.

I have seen some women who give their children that spot, that preeminence, in their affection, and thus crowd out the father. That is a serious mistake. Many marriages have failed for this very cause. They are partners, each given a part of the work of life to do. The fact that some

82

women and men disregard their work and their opportunities does not change the program.

The Lord said to the woman: "In sorrow thou shalt bring forth children." I wonder if those who translated the Bible might have used the term *distress* instead of sorrow. It would mean much the same, except I think there is great gladness in most Latter-day Saint homes when there is to be a child there. As he concludes this statement he says, "and thy desire shall be to thy husband, and he shall rule over thee." (Genesis 3:16.) I have a question about the word *rule.* It gives the wrong impression. I would prefer to use the word *preside,* because that's what he does. A righteous husband presides over his wife and family.

I have attended missionary meetings all over the world. I have heard thousands of missionaries tell about their families back home. I have heard the testimonies of these fine young men. What do they talk about? Almost invariably they speak of the faithfulness of their mothers, the devotion of their mothers to them, her training of them, her deep appreciation for them. Once in a while the father comes in for just a tiny word or two. As a father, I have felt a little twinge of jealousy sometimes when the missionary sons have thus expressed themselves; yet I know what these missionaries say is true and wholly justified. How happy the mothers must be with this adoration and love! Is it not worth all the "sorrow" and suffering and sacrifice?

We are happy to see Paul's exhortation to women. He instructed Titus to teach the women "to be discreet, chaste, keepers at home, good, obedient to their own husbands, that the word of God be not blasphemed." (Titus 2:5.) No woman has ever been asked by the Church authorities to follow her husband into an evil pit. She is to follow him as he follows and obeys the Savior of the world, but in deciding this, she should always be sure she is fair.

One woman said, "My home and husband come first

in my life. I took care of my children myself when they were little and trained them well. I taught them all to read at home." Here is a mother who is interested in more than just giving the child food and shelter.

Mothers have a sacred role. They are partners with God, as well as with their own husbands, first in giving birth to the Lord's spirit children, and then in rearing those children so they will serve the Lord and keep his commandments. Could there be a more sacred trust than to be a trustee for honorable, well-born, well-developed children? We affirm the Church's strong, unalterable stand against innovations or any unchastity or breaking of the laws that could possibly reflect in the lives of the children.

Motherhood is a holy calling, a sacred dedication for carrying out the Lord's work, a consecration and devotion to the rearing and fostering and the nurturing of body, mind, and spirit of those who kept their first estate and who came to this earth for their second estate to learn and be tested and to work toward godhood. The role of mother, then, is to help those children keep their second estate, so that they might have glory added upon their heads forever and ever.

We have often said that this divine service of motherhood can be rendered only by mothers. It may not be passed to others. Nurses cannot do it; public nurseries cannot do it. Hired help cannot do it; kind relatives cannot do it. Only by mother, aided as much as may be by a loving father, brothers and sisters, and other relatives, can the full needed measure of watchful care be given. The mother who entrusts her child to the care of others that she may do nonmotherly work, whether for gold, for fame, or for civic service, should remember that "a child left to himself bringeth his mother to shame." (Proverbs 29:15.)

And in the modern revelations we learn that if parents do not teach their children to pray and walk uprightly before the Lord, "the sin be upon the heads of the parents." (D&C 68:25.)

May God bless you sisters in your homes and in your families, and especially with your husbands that they may recognize in you a great power so that they might better fulfill their responsibilities in life. Your Heavenly Father will smile upon you as you live the commandments and teach them to your children. This is the work of the Lord. God Almighty is responsible for it. It is a great experience to put one's life in the hands of his Heavenly Father so that he may give the service that is required.

WOMAN'S ROLE IN
THE COMMUNITY

Elder Marvin J. Ashton

At the founding meeting of the Relief Society on March 17, 1842, President Joseph Smith addressed the sisters "to illustrate the object of the Society . . . to assist; by correcting the morals and strengthening the virtues of the community."

In outlining some of the duties of the Relief Society, President Brigham Young said the following:

"The sisters in our Female Relief Societies have done great good. Can you tell the amount of good that the mothers and daughters in Israel are capable of doing? No, it is impossible. And the good they will do will follow them to all eternity." (*Journal of Discourses* 13:34.)

"As I have often told my sisters in the Female Relief Societies, we have sisters here who, if they had the privilege of studying, would make just as good mathematicians or accountants as any man; and we think they ought to have the privilege to study these branches of knowledge that they may develop the powers with which they are endowed. We believe that women are useful, not only to sweep houses, wash dishes, make beds, and raise babies, but that they should stand behind the counter, study law or physic, or become good book-keepers and be able to do the business in any counting house, and all this to enlarge their sphere of usefulness for the benefit of society at large. In following these things they but answer the design of their creation." (JD 13:61.)

"Now, ladies, go to and organize yourselves into industrial societies. . . ." (JD 12:195.)

President Joseph F. Smith, in defining the purposes and duties of Relief Society, said: "I will speak of the Relief Society as one great organization in the Church . . . whose duty it is to look after the interests of all the women of Zion and of all the women that may come under their supervision and care, irrespective of religion, color or condition. . . . We want the young women, the intelligent women, women of faith, of courage and of purity, to be associated with the Relief Societies of the various Stakes and Wards of Zion. We want them to take hold of this work with vigor, with intelligence and unitedly, for the building up of Zion and the instruction of women in their duties—domestic duties, *public duties*, and every duty that may devolve upon them." (*Conference Report*, April 1907, p. 6.)

Later prophet-presidents of the Church have spoken similarly on women's role in community life.

These early endorsements by the prophets regarding women's responsibilities to community life came at a time when there were only faint stirrings on the part of women for greater participation in public life. In the main, woman's world was her home and family, her church, and limited voluntary service in her immediate community, such as nursing the sick, supporting church projects, and aiding in neighborhood community better-ment activities. Some women engaged in teaching children the three "R's"—reading, writing, and 'rithmetic. Often they did this as tutors in private homes. Today, woman's world is as broad as the universe is broad. There are few, if any, fields of human endeavor into which she may not enter if she has the will, the talent, and the skill to do so. Careers long closed to women are now opening and new careers are beckoning them. Thus, a new day dawns for women in regard to community life.

From the pen of Belle S. Spafford, general president of the Relief Society for more than twenty-nine years and former president of the National Council of Women, one of the truly great women in all of Church history, we glean the following:

"While good home and family life might be called the Mormon credo, inbred in Mormon women is a sense of responsibility to good community life and to orderly ways of meeting their community as well as their home responsibilities.

"With this pioneer heritage, our women have walked into the heritage of the nation—a nation that was the setting for the restoration of the gospel in this dispensation. Our legacy of industrious hands and sound guiding principles has helped plant vital seeds that have grown and flourished in national fields and from which good fruits now may be harvested. And this legacy has spread to other lands, wherever the Church may be found today. Mormon women must continue their planting, their cultivating, that the harvest may continue to be abundant and good." (*A Woman's Reach*, Deseret Book, 1974, p. 3.)

"A wise man has said that a sense of somebody's need is the most powerful motive in the world for worthy action; it appeals to the largest number of people of every age, race, and kind. It wakens the whole nature—the powers that learn as well as those that perform. It generates the vigor of interest that submerges selfishness. It arouses the inventiveness and ingenuity that slumber so soundly in the lives of so many people. For many of us, work that is service taps a great reservoir of power, sets free some of our caged and leashed energy, and rewards us with a deep-seated sense of satisfaction." (Ibid., p. 48.)

"Relief Society women will recall that the Prophet Joseph Smith admonished the sisters of Nauvoo to strengthen community virtues. We, today, would do well to heed this counsel. To be sure, we would do so in the manner approved by the Lord and his priesthood authorities.

"All too often one of our loved ones falls victim to attitudes and conditions in the community, at times even in the home, of which parents may be unaware, and engages in conduct that violates God's laws and the teachings of the Church. This is heartbreaking to parents. A wise present-day apostle has said: 'A child is never lost until his parents give up.' " (Ibid., p. 119.)

This change in the role of woman as an active participant with man in the work of the world had its beginning, according to many historians, in about 1833. This is of particular interest when one recalls that the Church was organized in 1830. From Sister Spafford, the same talented lady quoted above, we share the following:

"In the early part of the nineteenth century, Eli Whitney invented the cotton gin. It revived the slumping institution of slavery, which was growing increasingly distasteful to many women, who by nature were endowed with humanitarian impulses. Weaving came out of the home, taking with it numbers of women to work at the industrial power looms. The industrial revolution was being born. This and the distaste for slavery are generally regarded as being behind the stirrings of the women for greater freedom of action and better opportunities for education." ("The American Woman's Movement," an address delivered July 12, 1974, in New York, N.Y., p. 7.) This in turn provided that they might more fully develop personally, and thus be of greater usefulness.

Sister Spafford continues: "We recall . . . that [early in the 1900s] war had descended upon the world, World War I followed by World War II. The wars seemed to entice, if not force, women out of their homes and into the labor market. After World War II an interesting phenomenon occurred in the world of work. A good portion of the women who, as a patriotic duty during the war years, had taken jobs, many of which were traditionally uncommon to women, felt a new independence; they saw advantages in the paycheck, and many of them never went back to the home and the life of a full-time housewife." (Ibid., pp. 13-14.)

Other influences tended to take women out of their homes, to seek greater opportunities for education, service, and recognition. In 1842 the Prophet Joseph Smith, in organizing the Relief Society, turned the key in behalf of women. In 1848 a "Declaration of Independence for Women" was issued by the first Woman's

Rights Convention in Seneca Falls, New York. It demanded educational, industrial, social, and political rights for women. Then began the long struggle for more effectively organized groups of women who wished to obtain national suffrage. In the United States women were granted this suffrage with the adoption of the nineteenth amendment to the Constitution in 1920. Other influences that have led women into public life have been technological developments that have taken much of the drudgery out of the homes and have left women free to go into service outside the homes. In recent years the rise in the cost of living due to inflation has also influenced the decision of many women to seek additional earnings for their families through paid employment in the community.

These conditions have led women not only to seek better opportunities for education, but also greater recognition as community builders. Concern over the trend particularly as it might adversely affect home and family life has been recognized by serious-minded, leading women of the world. A voice of warning was sounded at the International Congress of Women held in Helsinki, Finland, in 1954. Dr. Jeanne Edar, president of the International Council of Women, stated at this conference, "Today's generations are fated to stand on the frontiers of this development [atomic energy] gazing with awe into a future destined to be very different from the past into which the atom will bring enormous new good or evil, unpredictable today and depending upon the use humanity will make of its powers."

She went on to point out that women must continue to carry out their duties as mothers, householders, educators, and the living consciences of their contemporaries. Then she asked if they would also accept new interests and duties in their communities in the working world, in their native lands, and in international relations. Dr. Edar referred to the present as a day that needs "our work, our meditation, and our choice of values." She urged the women to work together "in friendship and mutual support, led by sound reason, for the preservation of the home as a vital cornerstone of society and for the strengthening of moral and spiritual values in community life." She said that women have always been the "creators and preservers of life" and "a source of strength and calmness to their neighbors." Then she appealed to them to "continue in these roles, unsusceptible to the influences of propaganda that create fears and hysteria." (*Relief Society Magazine*, October 1954, pp. 650-51.)

Women with clear-sighted vision must see that the greatest contribution a woman can make to community life is to maintain a home where spiritual and ethical values are internalized in family members—a home from which will go forth responsible citizens dedicated to high moral standards, industrious work habits, love of God, and concern for fellowman.

Sister Spafford once reported on a manpower conference that she attended at Brigham Young University, where the keynote speaker made a strong plea for women to "go into the labor market well trained to strengthen the national economy." He stated that this was the most important contribution women could make to national life. Following his address Sister Spafford asked him which he felt was more important, a strong national economy or a strong national character. She herself then "expressed the opinion that I felt a strong national character was of first importance and that this was born and bred in the homes. If we had strong national character, I was of the opinion that a strong national economy would eventually follow."

A small political brochure titled "Utah Women Speak" makes the following statement concerning the position of women today: "We believe . . . that quality life for all is built on the foundation of good home and family life. If the home is in trouble, the community is in trouble. If the community is in trouble, the nation is in trouble. Therefore, we support . . . legislative and social actions which strengthen the home and protect and promote its stability. We oppose . . . any action that in any way threatens or adversely affects the home and family."

A solid family structure is the very foundation of every stable and permanent society.

Today in many affluent countries of the world there are philosophies, points of view, and patterns of life that are threatening the home and family as traditionally known, and as they have contributed to quality life for all. The threat is extending to our entire social structure. It is real, though all too often unrecognized as a threat. Marital relationships and family life are breaking down. Divorces are increasing alarmingly. Subtle influences are abroad to encourage young people of marriageable age to prefer alternatives to marriage vows and ceremonies, both religious and civil. There is agitation for more relaxed divorce laws. There is growing open discussion and acceptance of deviate relationships between men and women. Such expressions as "Patriarchal determined values must go" are common. Common also are such expressions as "eradicate the supremacy of male-approved desires and dominance."

Action born of spiritual values, such as volunteer service, would be curbed by some. One organized woman's group maintains that existing excessive volunteer service by women must go because the volunteer woman worker robs another woman who needs paid employment opportunities.

As times have changed, new demands on the part of women have come to the fore, and agitation that these be met is being intensified. There is growing evidence that the natural differences between men and women are all too often being disregarded. "Unisex" is becoming a popular word. Too many women are confused as to their priority roles in life. The glamorous enticement of a career outside the home is all too often taking precedence over the eternal joys of home and family life. Both home and family life and community service—either on a volunteer or paid basis—are within the grasp of the well-organized woman, each in its turn. A woman should feel free to go into the marketplace and into community service on a paid or volunteer basis if she so desires when her home and family circumstances allow her to do so without impairment to them.

This is a day when serious-minded, clear-thinking women are needed to promote a climate of peace, harmony, and righteousness in community life. Let such women work together to create an atmosphere in which the problems of our society can be resolved by reason, respect, and concern for all people, and by esteem for that which has traditionally proved conducive to mankind's happiness and well-being.

Let women exercise their hard-won voting franchise with intelligence, knowing about the candidates' position on the issues of concern to women. Let them make sure that they themselves are informed on the issues and their effect on the family and the community. Let there be a reaffirmation of the moral and social values set forth in the commandments of the Lord.

Let us remember that the woman whose life is well ordered may and should work for the benefit of both her community and her family. She contributes in two highly important ways: first, through bearing and rearing good citizens, and second, through upholding, exemplifying, and working toward high community standards as the circumstances of her life permit.

THE WOMEN
OF GOD

Elder Neal A. Maxwell

We know so little about the reasons for the division of duties between womanhood and manhood as well as between motherhood and priesthood. These were divinely determined in another time and another place. We are accustomed to focusing on the men of God because theirs is the priesthood and leadership line. But paralleling that authority line is a stream of righteous influence reflecting the remarkable women of God who have existed in all ages and dispensations, including our own. Greatness is not measured by coverage in column inches, either in newspapers or in the scriptures. Therefore, the story of the women of God is, for now, an untold drama within a drama.

We men know the women of God as wives, mothers, sisters, daughters, associates, and friends. You seem to tame us and to gentle us, and yes, to teach us and to inspire us. For you, we have admiration as well as affection, because righteousness is not a matter of role, nor goodness a matter of gender. In the work of the kingdom, men and women are not without each other, but do not envy each other, lest by reversals and renunciations of role we make a wasteland of both womanhood and manhood.

Just as certain men were foreordained from before the foundations of the world, so were certain women appointed to certain tasks. Divine design—not chance—brought Mary forward to be the mother of Jesus. The boy prophet, Joseph Smith, was blessed not only with a great father but also with a superb mother, Lucy Mack, who influenced a whole dispensation.

When we would measure loving loyalty in a human relationship, do we not speak of Ruth and Naomi even more than David and Jonathan? And no wonder God with his perfect regard for women is so insistent about our obligations to widows.

A widow with her mite taught us how to tithe. An impoverished and starving widow with her hungry son taught us how to share, as she gave her meal and oil to Elijah. The divine maternal instincts of an Egyptian woman retrieved Moses from the bulrushes, thereby shaping history and demonstrating how a baby is a blessing—not a burden.

What greater conversation of anticipation has there been than that of Elisabeth and Mary when also the babe in Elisabeth leaped in recognition of Mary? (Luke 1:41.) Does it not tell us much about the intrinsic intelligence of women to read of the crucifixion scene at Calvary? "And many women were there beholding afar off." (Matthew 27:55.) Their presence was a prayer; their lingering was like a litany.

And who came first to the empty tomb of the risen Christ? Two women. Who was the first mortal to see the resurrected Savior? Mary of Magdala. Special spiritual sensitivity keeps the women of God hoping long after many others have ceased.

The charity of good women is such that their "love makes no parade"; they are not glad "when others go wrong"; they are too busy serving to sit statusfully about, waiting to be offended. Like Mary, they ponder trustingly those puzzlements that disable others. God trusts women so much that he lets them bear and care for his spirit children.

In our modern kingdom, it is no accident that women were, through Relief Society, assigned compassionate service. So often the service of women seems instinctive, while that of some men seems more labored. It is precisely because the daughters of Zion are so uncommon that the adversary will not leave them alone.

We salute our sisters for the joy that is theirs as they rejoice in a baby's first smile and as they listen with eager ear to a child's first day at school, which bespeaks a special selflessness. Women, more quickly than others, will understand the possible dangers when the word *self* is militantly placed before other words like *fulfillment*. They rock a sobbing child without wondering if today's world is passing them by, because they know they hold tomorrow tightly in their arms.

So often our sisters comfort others when their own needs are greater than those being comforted. That quality is like the generosity of Jesus on the cross. Empathy during agony is a portion of divinity.

I thank the Father that his Only Begotten Son did not say in defiant protest at Calvary, "My body is my own!" I stand in admiration of women today who resist the fashion of abortion by refusing to make the sacred womb a tomb!

When the real history of mankind is fully disclosed, will it feature the echoes of gunfire—or the shaping sound of lullabies? The great armistices made by military men—or the peacemaking of women in homes and in neighborhoods? Will what happened in cradles and kitchens prove to be more controlling than what happened in congresses? When the surf of the centuries has made the great pyramids so much sand, the everlasting family will still be standing, because it is a celestial institution, formed outside telestial time. The women of God know this.

No wonder the men of God support and sustain our sisters in their unique roles, for the act of deserting home in order to shape society is like thoughtlessly removing crucial fingers from an imperiled dike in order to teach people to swim.

We men love them for meeting inconsiderateness with consideration, and selfishness with selflessness. We are touched by the eloquence of their example. We are deeply grateful for their enduring us as men when we are not at our best because—like God—they love us not only for what we are, but for what we have the power to become.

We have special admiration for the unsung but unsullied single women, among whom are some of the noblest daughters of God. These sisters know that God loves them, individually and distinctly. They make wise career choices even though they cannot have the most choice career. Though in their second estate they do not have their first desire, they still overcome the world. These sisters who cannot now enrich the institution of their own marriage so often enrich other institutions in society. They do not withhold their blessings simply because some blessings are now withheld from them. Their trust in God is like that of the wives who are childless, not by choice, but who in the justice of God will receive special blessings one day.

To wives who, for one reason or another, cannot have children of their own—but who love and care enough to reach out through the process of adoption to make deserving children their own—our admiration is also expressed. Childless wives can render much significant service to the children of our Father in heaven even if they cannot, naturally or through adoption, have children of their own.

I, along with my brethren of the priesthood, express undying gratitude to our eternal partners. We know that we can go no place that matters without you, nor would we have it otherwise. When we kneel to pray, we kneel together. When we kneel at the altar of the holy temple, we kneel together. When we approach the final gate where Jesus himself is the gatekeeper, we will, if faithful, pass through that gate together.

The prophet who presides over us today could tell us of such togetherness, when at the time of his overwhelming apostolic calling he was consoled by his Camilla, who met his anguished, sobbing sense of inadequacy and, running her fingers through his hair, said, "You can do it, you can do it." He surely has done it, but with her at his side.

May our brethren notice how all the prophets treat

97

their wives and honor women, and let us do likewise!

Finally, remember: When we return to our real home, it will be with the "mutual approbation" of those who reign in the "royal courts on high." There we will find beauty such as mortal eye hath not seen; we will hear sounds of surpassing music which mortal ear hath not heard. Could such a regal homecoming be possible without the anticipatory arrangements of a Heavenly Mother?

Meanwhile, there are no separate paths back to that heavenly home. There is just one straight and narrow way, at the end of which, though we arrive trailing tears, we shall at once be "drenched in joy."

"MAGIC APLENTY"

Elder Marion D. Hanks

A few years ago I became acquainted with a young American Indian attorney who had been born and brought up on a reservation in the northeast part of the United States. His delightful sense of humor enlivened discussions underway concerning various survey and field studies relating to youth. He said that one summer he and a friend from the reservation had set out to study the people who were studying Indians. In that one summer they investigated investigators who were working in sixty-four different studies of Indian tribes! The report was that those who were studying Indians were quite surprised to find themselves being studied by Indians.

Occasionally I have thought of this man and his experience as I have talked with various single adults in the Church. While there are those among them who feel that much more attention and consideration should be given them, there are others who would prefer that single adults not be separated out from the rest of the community and made to feel that they are exceptional and need special attention.

The fact is, however, that the role of single men and women brings additional challenges, and that is especially true for single women in the Church.

Some of the special problems for the single woman who is a faithful believer in the gospel of Jesus Christ are reflected in the following brief extracts from statements made by choice Latter-day Saint women of various circumstances.

Being 32 and not married has some aspects of pain known only to the single Mormon woman. As I begin to write this I am crying. My dreams seem so unattainable. But the dreams are not unusual or grandiose. They seem so simple in my mind. I hunger to be happily married. Where do I go with these dreams? . . .

Maybe it is this need to "be lovable" that becomes the pain inside us. In the mind of society there must be a reason when one is not married. What is the flaw in me?

A lady who is widowed adds:

It is better for us, I think, than for the divorced or never married. We have loved and been loved, and though we become desperately lonely for the one who has gone, yet we feel married still, and still loved as we continue to love.

Of the problems of a divorced woman, one has said:

Divorced Mormons often become alienated from the Church entirely. For those who cling vigorously to the source of blessings rather than cutting themselves off, there is yet the sometimes present problem of uneasy fellow members who regard divorced people as having something wrong with them, perhaps something contagious, like a disease, and who do not know how to act with such a one who may be innocent of any wrongdoing, even victimized.

To these sobering comments is added one from an unexpected source. A faithful Latter-day Saint who married out of the Church, with hopes for a future she no longer feels will come to pass, expresses a viewpoint that may surprise some. She writes about a particular kind of singleness.

I have always been a member of the Church and was active (did not miss a meeting, held three jobs at a time, etc.) up to the very day of my marriage. I married a Catholic. (Go ahead and wince. I am still kind of shocked at myself at such an incredible complete flip!) With this in mind, I thought I would mention that one version of the single woman in the Church is the woman who married a nonmember. You know—the woman who really believed all those faith-promoting stories on conversion would happen to her. They have not. They may not. She is no longer the unattached sister. Her hard-core non-believer is very real and loving, but not Golden Question material after all. She is alone. Sitting. Sensitive. Weeping (inside). Never wanting to give up hope; never seeing it either. It can be psychologically devastating to realize that you are now numbered among the inactive. You are still somebody's ward project. You are downing the percentages in all the books. Still, you have a testimony. You certainly think about the Church all the time. If you have ever practiced love, charity, humility, and studied the gospel in your home, it has been these married years—alone.

A candid summation to these observations was supplied by one of the above women:

The Church is not only family-oriented, but it is also couple-oriented. One who lives the life of the gospel, being a single adult, must be content with these feelings and battle to be happy in spite of them.

This is true, of course. The traditional anticipated role of woman in the Church is as a partner in marriage, as a wife, mother, homemaker, and the heart of a family. This will forever be so. The Church will continue to emphasize the importance of home and family and of the role of parents in that setting. Honorable motherhood will always be regarded as the highest blessing and privilege of the daughters of God. Emphasis will surely continue to be given to the important nature of the home and the vital meaning of the family in preserving and building a society that is constructive and worthwhile. Temple marriage will be held out as a lofty objective for every member of the Church. Preparation for that kind of marriage will be strongly encouraged, and instructions and example will be provided that will help to qualify people for that holy experience.

But all of this must not and will not be done insensitively and without the tender consciousness that there are many wonderful women in the society and in the Church who have not enjoyed or do not now enjoy the blessings of marriage and family in the traditional way. Many who are eligible have not married. There are the widowed and the divorced, and among these are many who head one-parent families. Circumstances in these several groups differ as do the conditions of individuals within the groups, and what may well be fitting for one person may not be well-suited for another. Nonetheless, there are some principles and ideas to be considered that relate to all women in all circumstances.

Every woman is special, a somebody of intrinsic worth who has been a somebody for a very long time, indeed forever. Every child of God, born of divine heritage in the spirit before this world was formed, enters mortal life already a special eternal person. Each has already proved herself in lengthy and demanding periods of trial, has chosen the right course and pursued it with faith and courage, and comes here with credentials earned in action elsewhere.

Every girl, every woman, is a somebody, apart and aside from anyone else, husband or family or otherwise. If she is privileged to enjoy fruitful family association in this world—happy marriage and motherhood and the challenge of children—then she is favored indeed, and through obedience to the laws of the Lord she qualifies for the eternal union and all the other choice blessings that are promised for every faithful child of God who desires them and is willing to receive them.

If the anticipated timetable for establishing a base for those blessings is delayed in this world, or if the base, once established, is disrupted, the promises still pertain: ". . . all that God hath" can be hers if she desires it and lives for it.

In a sense, the old couplet about sin is also true of exaltation: "The sins we do by two and two / We must pay for one by one."

Eternal life, life with God, life of divine quality, creative progressive life—exaltation—is a loving life shared with dear ones, but we must qualify for it one by one. The ultimate enjoyment of this level of life is the consequence of individual choice in accepting, through obedience to his commandments, the invitation of the Lord to be with him and our other loved ones everlastingly.

The trail to earthly and eternal happiness always leads back to the individual and the way each uses her agency. The prophet Lehi taught that God's children are "free according to the flesh; and all things are given them which are expedient unto man. And they are free to choose liberty and eternal life [through Christ], or to choose captivity and death. . . ." (2 Nephi 2:27.)

Perhaps the major factor in guiding our choices is our feeling about ourselves, about who we are. Socrates said, "The ignorance which causes vice and immorality is not ignorance of moral principles or laws, but an ignorance of self."

In the wonderful musical *Fiddler on the Roof* Tevye explains that the strength of their beleaguered lives is possible because "everyone knows who he is and what God expects him to do."

What is man? Who are we? Is it so vital that we know? What does God expect of us? In an interview, Rabbi Abraham Joshua Heschel replied: "For the person who understands his own nature, the challenge and the joy in life are in learning how rich life can be and what an endless opportunity for doing the good and the holy."

What is our "own nature"? The apostle Paul taught the Romans: "The Spirit itself beareth witness with our spirit, that we are the children of God: And if children, then heirs; heirs of God, and joint-heirs with Christ. . . ." (Romans 8:16-17.)

His testimony to the men of Athens on Mars Hill was that we are all the "offspring of God." (Acts 17:28-29.)

Each of us is three things:

1. A child of God, a spiritual being.

2. A sister or brother to all others of God's children.

3. A person, an individual, in the long process of maturation toward eternal creative stature.

Eternity gives mortal time its meaning. Knowing our

true nature and using our time and agency in honoring our origins and promise by developing our capacities in all three aspects of our nature is the major purpose of mortality. Possessing a mortal body, understanding it to be a part of our eternal soul, we undertake to grow—as God's child, as a sister and neighbor, and as an individual on an exciting eternal journey, with our own fate and future carried within us.

1. Child of God

Faith is the force of fulfillment for each of us. For a single woman making a life of learning and giving and loving, faith is not a definition, but a condition of confidence in God, held in the mind and heart of a seeking and believing child. It is not perfect knowledge, as the prophets repeatedly teach us, but it *is* knowing some things very well. It is not present perfection of behavior, but a commitment to the goal at the end of the difficult road of repentance and forgiveness and growth, which is to *become* perfect. It is not the guarantee of an easy life, but the source of power to endure tribulations and trials with the promise of ultimate victory. Faith is to know that God will never reject us: that we need not "hang down our heads, for we are not cast off" (2 Nephi 10:20); that he is gracious, forgiving, and loving unto even the most undeserving of us, and that "therefore will the Lord wait, that he may be gracious unto you, and therefore will he be exalted, that he may have mercy upon you." (Isaiah 30:18.)

A young lady, anguished in aloneness, cried out, "Heavenly Father, do you know I am here?" She shyly shared the experience with others later, and some who heard did not comprehend the sincerity and intensity of her quest. In tears she told them, "Maybe it doesn't sound like so big a deal to you, but I'd like you to know that I know that he knows that I am here."

Sufficient strength for the task or the day and capacity to cope lie in sincere search and study, in loving and giving of self, in serving, in fasting and prayer and faith in God's love and the sure triumph of his purposes and program for his children.

Robert Louis Stevenson wrote of the frantic fear of the youngster who locked himself in a closet. His father was summoned. "When I heard the voice of my father," the youth said, "panic ceased. The dark was still there, but there was no fear."

Tolstoi said, "God lives. I know—I talked with Him this morning."

Strength and serenity follow faith—confidence in God—and come with knowing who we are.

Long ago in Book of Mormon times, a prophet sought to help but was "without hope" for a group of unrepentant sinful people who "did struggle for their lives without calling upon that Being who created them." (Mormon 5:2.)

Every daughter of God has need to call upon him and to know that in Christ there is strength for every challenge. Listen to the promise of Mormon, recorded in Moroni 8:25-26:

. . . the fulfilling the commandments bringeth remission of sins; And the remission of sins bringeth meekness, and lowliness of heart; and because of meekness and lowliness of heart cometh the visitation of the Holy Ghost, which Comforter filleth with hope and perfect love, which love endureth by diligence unto prayer, until the end shall come, when all the saints shall dwell with God.

The power of faith in Christ's love can transform human life from a dreary struggle without meaning into a joyous adventure.

2. Sister and Neighbor

In acts of unselfishness and service lie sanity and the capacity to endure and conquer. The centuries have not dimmed, but indeed have deeply demonstrated, the validity of the admonition of the Lord that forgetting ourselves, losing our lives for others in his name and spirit, is always and forever the path to saving our lives. It is said often and believed widely but practiced too infrequently. Perhaps we do not know or think we do not know how to "lose" ourselves. Yet in the course of a lifetime we have seen enough and learned enough to know that in quiet rooms and humble homes and hospitals and sometimes hovels, in jungle outposts and mission centers, in places far and near, selfless acts of kindness and love go on. Sometimes we have waited too long to learn and appreciate and emulate such service and those who give it, yet in the highways and byways we have come to know of the unsung heroism and sweet Christlike self-forgetfulness of humble folk. They teach us the lesson all over again, and with more force than pulpit pronouncements.

We are neighbor to all men, including those nearest—perhaps in the next room or through the wall or block, certainly in the neighborhood and always in the community.

After surviving a concentration camp in World War II, the admired Lutheran pastor Martin Niemoller wrote the following of his experience with the Gestapo: "They came for the Jews, and I was not a Jew so I did not object. Then they came for the Catholics, and I was not a Catholic so I did not object. Then they came for the trade unionists, and I was not a trade unionist so I did not object. Then they came for me and there was nobody left to object."

When his great nation fell in World War II, the French marshal Henri Petain, earlier an authentic war hero and celebrated savior of his country, went down with it, and later explained why he and his people succumbed: "Our spirit of enjoyment was stronger than our spirit of sacrifice. We wanted to have *more* than we wanted to *give*. We tried to spare effort and we met disaster."

Self-pity is a mortal enemy, and preoccupation with self is a form of surrender to our own imperfect circumstances. Exclusive attention to our own needs at the expense of our opportunity as a neighbor is tragedy. We are meant to give, all of us, and a single woman who may feel deprived or distressed can save herself sorrow and overcome aloneness and hopelessness by serving and giving. It is indispensable to our survival and success that we give and receive love, that we think ourselves worthwhile to ourselves and others.

The fondest memories of my early childhood are related to home and the little hearth in front of the tiny fireplace that seemed so strong a symbol of security in the midst of very limited material comforts, and to the cozy kitchen warmed by a coal stove and filled with fetching fragrances of fresh bread and Mother's special chili or stew or vegetable pie. From this sanctuary we could venture forth at bedtime into cold bedrooms to be enveloped in frigid covers that soon warmed to our shivering selves. Beyond those very special memories, enjoyed no doubt by many, are the settings-forth to share. We were a one-parent family. Mother had to work to provide for us, and she had responsibilities in Relief Society, but they were only a formalized part of her humanity. I sensed then and certainly know now that much of her strength and, I have no doubt, some of her capacity to care for us temporally as well as spiritually came through the principle of sending forth succor on the waters, and having it return in added measure.

Still and always it will be true that getting one's mind off one's self and the requirements of the day, motivated by the discovered needs of others and the earnest effort to serve, will surely bless and strengthen any sincere soul. And the giving need not always or primarily be of material things. Food and clothing are critical for those who do not have enough, but so are kindness and encouragement, time to listen and understand, caring and concern.

I attended a gathering of single parents recently. We laughed and wept together and shared our feelings. The most uplifting thing about the experience, to me, was the number of those present who came to me after to mention the special problems or heartbreak of others, to ask a blessing for them, or to seek strength for them through prayer or a note or a word of concern.

God loves all his children, but he needs instruments for the revelation and expression of his love. We are most blessed when we are most useful, and any life will demonstrate the validity of the principle that manifests, in its giving of self, an understanding of that principle.

3. A Person

It is our responsibility to be merciful and compassionate in our relationships with others, to value them, and to be respectful of and defend their rights to their own convictions and priorities of value. But we can do this more completely and honestly when we know and value our own selves and seek to develop and improve our gifts and talents. Self-respect and self-esteem are the products of good self-image. Our own perceptions of our self in body, mind, and spirit are critical to the enjoyment of life and to our contributions to life.

Respect and appreciation for the body and proper care of it are marks of wisdom and maturity and faith. Many of our physical ills are self-inflicted. The simple reality is that we are guardians of our own health as well as our own character, and in the ultimate, the whole of our lives.

The ancient Greeks taught that the combination of strong body and sound mind is the resource for all others of life's blessings and contributions, and in the gospel of Jesus Christ this union is eternal and universal—"The body and spirit are the soul of man." (D&C 88:15.)

The whole system of psychosomatic medicine has grown on the concept that mind and body work inseparably and each affects the other significantly and inevitably. Vigorous physical exercise is a widely prescribed treatment for depression and mental illness. To keep our bodies from the ill effects of substances and actions that are destructive is basic, but beyond that are the positive efforts required for constructive strengthening of the body.

Recently I spoke with one of the best and most beautiful persons I know, who has been confined to a wheelchair for nearly twoscore years. She has undergone difficulty and pain that are beyond the comprehension of those who have not suffered it. Yet she was earnestly expressing thanks to God for this body which has permitted her to live and breathe in this world and is the subject of God's promises of perfection and glorification and renewal and cleansing in the world to come. I sat marveling as she with absolute sincerity thanked God for her body, the earthly and eternal housing of her spirit. Its present infirmity she has painfully endured, but it has served as her tabernacle here and she loves and honors it and looks forward to the time of its perfection.

What a remarkable and inspiring attitude!

If this great soul can regard her body with appreciation, understanding and valuing it and finding it useful and beautiful, all the rest of us should also. For any choice daughter of God the maximum effort to keep active, to build a strong base of good and vibrant health, to work hard at conditioning and developing a healthy and attractive body all are especially important. The elements of that effort are the same for everyone.

First, physical activity is essential to good health. One of the nation's leading experts on health, a physician, notes, "Exercise is the most significant factor contributing to the health of the individual." Regular, energetic, appropriate physical exercise is an indispensable key to good condition and good health.

A President of the United States has written of the broad effects of physical activity: "We have reached a new understanding of the role of exercise and sports in our lives. Regular, vigorous physical activity provides a pleasant and relaxing way of filling leisure hours. But more than this, it enhances health, improves mental and physical performance, and even helps to prolong life. It is folly to lead a sedentary existence when so much enjoyment and so many benefits can be gained from the active life." (Gerald R. Ford.)

Someone who is in close touch with professional basketball and has a keen sense of what goes on in the world recently noted that most of us wake up in the morning with pressures already upon us roughly akin to the Boston full-court press! For the athletically uninitiated, that means a large amount of pressure. With pollution threatening our physical environment and with large numbers of people involved in too much smoke, drink, food, and stress—indeed, too much of everything except vigorous physical activity—the health prognosis of the general populace is not promising.

Second, what we eat—its nature, quality, and the quantity of it—is of great importance to our health. Sufficient information is available to permit anyone to qualify as an expert of sorts in selecting proper food in appropriate amounts. As to weight, the simple truth is that if we consume more calories than we expend, we gain weight; if we consume less than we expend, we lose weight.

We should never *eat* more calories in a day than we *use* in a day. The excess adds up to fat and fat adds up to obesity, and obesity is a serious health hazard. The price of every pound of fat is a shorter life expectancy.

Third, we differ in our specific requirements, but every human being needs an adequate amount of sleep regularly to be healthy. The Lord has told us: "See that ye love one another; cease to be covetous; learn to impart one to another as the gospel requires. Cease to be idle; cease to be unclean; cease to find fault one with another; cease to sleep longer than is needful; retire to thy bed early, that ye may not be weary; arise early, that your bodies and your minds may be invigorated." (D&C 88:123-24.)

Fourth, the human system needs a break from the ordinary and customary schedules of work and pressure. Recreation that brings rest and relaxation is vital. It need not be expensive or complicated or lengthy.

Fifth, personal cleanliness is important to physical health and attractiveness. Meticulous care of ourself and our living place and possessions is a hallmark of self-respect and wisdom.

Sixth, a cheerful and constructive and courageous attitude based on a sense of appreciation for life and delight in it is the thread that runs through a healthful approach to living.

Each of these matters is something that the individual can decide upon and govern in her life.

The mind, too, needs exercise. It needs to stretch and reach and expand and develop. Activity is essential to mental alertness. In our individual program of personal growth, the improvement of the mind is basic. The mind thrives on a variety of interests. The outreach that moves us to seek for new experiences and deeper understanding, that prompts reading and studying, thinking, and meditating, can lead us to learn things and to involve ourselves in well-chosen activities that will be exciting and productive.

Joseph Addison long ago wrote: "Reading is to the mind what exercise is to the body. As by the one, health is preserved, strengthened and invigorated; by the other, virtue, (which is the health of the mind) is kept alive, cherished and confirmed."

One who doesn't read good books on his own volition is living in a state of cultural deprivation. What someone has called the "Three C's: Comics, Condensations, and Concoctions," are starvation fare—or maybe worse—for a mind that is meant for substance and will thrive on the energy available in good literature.

For the seeking, alert mind, the world is full of joy and beauty and excitement. Sometimes we have too few "pictures on the wall," as it were, and sometimes too many. We can become slaves to pursuing, to possessing, to having. If there are too many, we see cracks in the frames and dust on them; we try to straighten them or think of better ways to arrange them, but it is possible we do not really see them.

David Grayson, in the book *Great Possessions*, talked to this intent with a lady and then said to her, "I see now why you have just one rose on your table." "Yes," she responded eagerly, "isn't it a beauty! I spent half an hour this morning looking for the best and most perfect rose in the garden and there it is." We need to look widely, but also to be discriminating.

It is also important to be alive to what is around us. From an unknown source comes this testament: "Life is what we are alive to. It is not length but breadth. To be alive only to appetite, pleasure, pride, moneymaking, and not to goodness and kindness, purity and love, history, poetry, music, flowers, stars, God and eternal hope, is to be all but dead."

The mind is a magnificent instrument that in many of us is scarcely used. It can be fed, exercised, filled, emptied, stretched, and disciplined. It is the seat of content and the source of strength. Samuel Johnson gave it a respectful summation: "The fountain of content must spring up in the mind, and he who has so little knowledge of human nature as to seek happiness by changing anything but his own disposition will waste his life in fruitless efforts and multiply the griefs which he purposes to remove."

Women Who Have Not Married

There are women who do not choose to marry and who in their own view have sound reasons why they should not. Mental or physical health problems are present in some instances. Home or family burdens may enmesh. Educational or professional pursuits or just earning a living preoccupy others. Expectations that may be too high, or uncertainty in responding to opportunities, limit some. For others the timetable and appropriate occasion have just not come about. For all of these and others who may not have married for yet different reasons, the fact of singleness exists and must be dealt with. The faithful single woman reads in sacred writ that marriage under God's law is required of those who inherit the fulness of his blessings in the celestial kingdom. She is not married and thus many times feels that she can never qualify, that this door is shut to her.

Not so! The promises of God remain fast and certain, and they will be fulfilled sometime somewhere for every one of his children who desires them and qualifies. Nothing is more clear than that the Almighty is a God of "lovingkindness, judgment [justice], and righteousness in the earth." One of the sweetest and tenderest of modern proverbs is this, penned by a wise and lovely unmarried daughter of God: "To believe in God is to know that all the rules will be fair and that there will be wonderful surprises."

Wisdom and reason and faith cry out that no promise of God will be withheld from any willing child of God who for reasons beyond her own choosing or making does not and cannot meet the established requirements in this mortal life.

The prophets have said it and repeated it. A thought or two among many should suffice to settle the matter finally and put to rest any anxiety in the mind of every person who needs the assurance.

President Spencer W. Kimball has said: ". . . insofar as eternity is concerned, . . . no soul will be deprived of rich, eternal blessings for anything which that person could not help . . . and that the Lord never fails in his promises and that every righteous woman will receive eventually all to which she is entitled which she has not forfeited through any fault of her own. [A faithful woman] can lean heavily upon the promises of our Heavenly Father." (Special Interest Fireside, December 29, 1974.)

Elder Melvin J. Ballard stated: "Now then, what of your daughters who have died and have not been sealed to some man? . . . The sealing power shall be forever and ever with this church, and provisions will be made for them. . . . Their blessings and privileges will come to them in due time." ("Three Degrees of Glory," discourse delivered in the Ogden Tabernacle, September 2, 1922.)

But the promised blessings do not just *happen*. They are not automatic. They are brought about through faith and obedience and endurance in trial, just as every blessing is enjoyed through obedience to that law upon which it is predicated. Problems may be multiplied for single women, but they represent only a different form of challenge and indeed of trial and affliction. Troubles are the common experience of humankind and are not limited to the single person; theirs differ in some ways from the challenges laid upon others in other circumstances, but they are part of the program of mortal experience for everyone.

I think frequently of my fifth grade teacher at whose funeral I spoke and in response to whose request I bore testimony of appreciation for the warm and full and wonderful life she had led. She had not married, though she had earnestly desired to, but she was certain and wished it said that there awaited her the fulfillment of every blessing available to any of God's children if she faithfully and courageously did all she could to obey his commandments. Her life as a teacher was devoted to blessing the children of others, and brought her rich rewards. She never lost interest in any of "her" children. Through a lifetime often involving trials and difficulties, she fought the good fight, discovering "tongues in trees, sermons in stones, books in running brooks, and good in everything." She made this life full and lovely through her unselfish service and earnest effort, and none who knew her could doubt that the future that she now experiences has and will bring every rich blessing to her.

God's purposes and his children's righteous plans are

not abrogated or eternally short-circuited by frustration of our honest ambitions and desires.

Divorce

As noted in the statement quoted earlier from a divorced person, a divorcee who is a member of the Church is likely to encounter grave difficulties, and this is true whether or not any major flaw or fault instrumental in the divorce attaches to her. We have not fully looked this fact in the face, perhaps, but it is real and needs to be confronted. The divorced person herself can and must do much to meet a trying circumstance. But she needs help through the organization and programs of the Church, and particularly from individual members who, while they look upon divorce as a generally sad and undesirable occurrence, do not therefore condemn or reject the divorced person.

An individual who has suffered a divorce has undergone the loss of a loved one without much or any hope or promise of a future with that once-adored former mate. She loses both the one who has loved her and the one she has loved and served, and the effect is traumatic in the extreme. If the former husband initiated the divorce, then the rejection often is the more severe. Self-image is destructively impaired, associations with friends and the in-law family are usually jeopardized, life patterns are completely disrupted, finances often become a burdensome anxiety, the accustomed sweetheart relationship no longer exists, the partnership is dissolved, and (especially in the Church) the fellow disciple who shared purposes and principles and programs is gone. There are no manuals or classes on how to be divorced. The divorcee enters into a lonely and frightening unanticipated future, and it is extremely difficult.

If there are children, then the complexity is incredibly increased. Children have their own lives to live, and for the sake of a normal future they must be given every balancing opportunity to love the departed father, however much he may have been at fault. A one-parent family is basically incomplete. A little boy growing up in a home where a divorced mother habitually demeans or criticizes the absent parent may not think it very wholesome to be a male. A little girl who undergoes the same pressures may decide that men are not acceptable as partners, not to be trusted. In a one-parent family the conscientious mother is responsible for her children twenty-four hours a day, with no one to share with and no one to relieve the pressures and problems. Often she must work to supply the needs of the family, and this intensifies the challenge.

If in addition to all of this the divorced woman is looked upon with such unease that her condition is regarded as a threatening, communicable disease, then the pressures may indeed become unbearable, the depression near mortal, and the discouragement persistent.

Home teaching can be a significant help. Genuinely interested home teachers can add a dimension in a family where, we are reminded, not only the mother is divorced, but the children are divorced also. Wisdom and maturity are especially necessary.

One choice Latter-day Saint divorced woman, whose unfaithful husband walked away and made alliance with another, battled her heartbreak and all the problems attending her circumstance, suffered miserably, and found little acceptance or help until her bishop asked her to speak in sacrament meeting. She was not expected to talk about the details of her divorce or the specific circumstances of her problems. But she was asked to tell a bit about her own background, her life, and herself. As she spoke of the challenges that existed in her life and the lives of her youngsters, the warmth and purity of her soul touched the congregation. They began to change, she said, and from then on she was treated as a person whose problems and particular set of circumstances did not disqualify her from the affection and friendship and association of the "normal" individuals and families. She was accepted and responded to as the wholesome person she is, and her life and the lives of her children were appreciably blessed in a way they had before missed.

A sobering statement from this wise person is particularly revealing.

My family and friends who resented my husband's unfaithfulness and the subsequent divorce were very angry when they saw me hurt and knew in part the intensity of my suffering. They sought some kind of revenge to get back at the person who had hurt me. They would say, "Don't have anything to do with him. He is supposed to support the children so don't let him get away with a thing. I hope he gets a chance to suffer."

This is the last thing we need to hear. We need your strength; we need your positive view of life. We need to be reassured of God's love and justice to all his children. We need help in living the gospel of love in a very difficult, mixed-up time. Instead of saying those negative things, we need to hear "Try to work out the best possible relationship with your former husband. If you could live and have children with him, you can try to make the best divorced relationship for the sake of your children, yourself, and for your spouse." Help him to be a better parent by providing reinforcement and encouragement when possible. Help your children in a realistic way to accept him as he is, and not accept his sins. Be grateful and appreciative for what he does do. Pray for his happiness and success. If you can do this you will relieve yourself of the burden of judgment and punishment.

Such wisdom is unfortunately too rare.

The pressures on a divorced person in terms of dating and mating are perhaps greater than those experienced by other single persons. Attitude, self-image, principles all must be intensely safeguarded and reinforced. Predators seek prey among such, but even the noblest and purest character needs to walk carefully and to act wisely and with special restraint when the rivers of fire are invoked. Inhibition is not unhealthy but is indeed the keystone of civilized relationships, and a wise divorced person will move with care in forming and pursuing associations with others.

The best antidote to loneliness is still a life based on faith in God and Christ, filled with unselfish concern and service to others, and blessed with good and loyal friends who accept and actively include her in their lives, and who give help and encouragement in living the gospel of love. Activities and pursuits that are physically, socially, culturally, and spiritually productive are a blessing to be sought.

Widow

The impact of the loss of a beloved husband in death is one that can scarcely be imagined and is certainly not understood by one who has not encountered that ordeal. And yet, of the varied forms of singleness, there would seem to be here more solace and a more specific future than in any other. The gospel of Jesus Christ absolutely attests to the everlasting union of those married under God's holy order of matrimony. Lives lived with an active relationship to the covenants of that marriage will have been lives of preparation, joy, growth, increase, and eternal anticipation. A happy union will have stored a great reservoir of happy memories and a greater one of happy expectations. In the death of the mortal body and the passing on of the loved one, there is no break in the continuity of the spirit—not one parenthetic hour—nor is there any loss of love or loss of respect or loss of pride. Love goes on, grows, remains real, with every other really worthwhile thing, and the future becomes not just a fond dream, but an ever-intensifying reality.

Heartbreak is real, too—sorrow in separation, loss of companionship, aloneness. And problems are real: finances; family care and future where there are children; perhaps complexities with businesses or enterprises; new plans and relationships; perhaps at some future time, where appropriate, the possibility of a new alliance.

In all of these, all of the blessings of the gospel and of the Church are at hand to comfort and strengthen, and all of the pleasant and wholesome blessings of God's wonderful world are at hand to enjoy. To suffer through the incredible sorrow of separation is normal, to miss with deep heartbreak the daily presence of the beloved is normal, and to proceed slowly to reconciliation and wisdom is normal. He is not lost; he lives and loves and awaits you still. God lives and loves you still. In Christ there is strength for any need. In obedience and faithful service and unselfish love and concern there is added balm for one's own soul. In constant prayerfulness, frequent prayer, extended prayer there is peace and solace. And in fruitful, productive use of time there is great satisfaction and joy. With God, time is not. With mankind, "Art is long and life is fleeting."

In Shakespeare's *The Tempest* Miranda speaks of the "brave new world." Hercule Poirot, in a detective novel by Agatha Christie, is asked whether there is such a place. "There is always a brave new world," he replies, "but only for very special people. The lucky ones. The ones who carry the makings of that world within themselves."

Every woman carries within herself those "makings," but many of us are described by Matthew Arnold in *Empedocles on Etna:* "We would have inward peace / But will not look within."

Joy, strength, and our own future are all within us, not "out there" someplace. "We ourselves," wrote James Allen, "are makers of ourselves by virtue of the thoughts which we choose and encourage . . . mind is the master weaver, both of the inner garment of character and the outer garment of circumstances. . . ." (*As a Man Thinketh.*)

This is what the Lord offered us with the admonition to let virtue garnish our thoughts unceasingly and to fill ourselves with charity "to the household of faith" and toward all men. To enjoy the wonderful promised blessings, we must battle to keep in our minds that which is courageous, compassionate, merciful, hopeful, cheerful, and constructive. Sickly, bitter, and impure thoughts must be washed from our mind and not permitted to festoon its walls or fill its file drawers. Such thoughts come, and they come with special frequency and force in the dark and despairing hours, but they must be resisted at the walls and banished when they penetrate, because they carry their own destructive effect and can indeed destroy our peace and productive power if we admit them or entertain them as acceptable guests.

The best in us is better than we know, and must be sought for in faith and prayer, brought to the surface, and expressed in thought and action. Henry Thoreau used to lie in bed for a while in the morning telling himself all the good news he could think of, that he had a healthy body, that his mind was alert, that his work was interesting, that the future looked bright, that a lot of people trusted him. Presently he arose to meet the day in a world filled for him with good things, good people, good opportunities.

As usual, the scriptures sum up in a few words the truth of the matter. When John the Baptist heard of Christ's miracles, including the restoration to life of the son of the widow at Nain, he sent messengers to inquire of Christ, and they returned with Christ's answer. Then the Lord spoke to the people about John, repeating to them three times the words: "What went ye out for to see?" So much depends upon what we are looking for, what we expect, what we are alive to. Attitude is of critical importance.

Obedience is and forever will be the path to good conscience, and good conscience is the product of a life that merits its own approbation because it is moving toward meritorious goals with repentance, self-forgiveness, integrity, and growing strength. Keep the commandments! David Starr Jordan wrote that every true worthy child of God has learned: "There is no real excellence in all this world that can be separated from right living." Gandhi said, "My life is my message."

Mature single women need to face the sobering warning of Dr. Will Durrant, who wrote:

After hunger, sex is the strongest instinct and the greatest passion . . . sex becomes such a fire and a flame in the blood that it can burn up the whole personality which should be a hierarchy of harmony and desires. Today's society has over-stimulated the sexual impulse. Where our ancestors played down the sex instinct, knowing that it was strong enough without encouragement, we have blown it up with a thousand forms of advertisement and display.

Then we have armed sex with the doctrine that inhibition is dangerous. History shows that inhibition, the control of impulse, is the first principle of civilization.

One does not refrain from loving; one sublimates love and expresses it wisely and widely. A woman doesn't need to be married to love: she needs to be a true instrument of God's love, and she will then find love as she gives it. In the end, happiness can be found in self-fulfillment, which comes, as do other marvelous and mysterious blessings from God, with self-forgetfulness in love of God and our neighbors. You can fill a life by being thoughtful, dignify a life by being unselfish, and sanctify a life by committing energies to being God's instrument of love to his children.

Joseph Smith said: "Let every one labor to prepare himself for the vineyard, sparing a little time to comfort the mourners; to bind up the broken-hearted; to reclaim the backslider; to bring back the wanderer; to reinvite into the kingdom such as have been cut off . . . to work righteousness, and, with one heart and one mind, prepare to help redeem Zion, that goodly land of promise where the willing and obedient shall be blessed." (History of the Church 2:228-29.)

Francis Thompson in *Hound of Heaven* gave us a line every daughter of God needs to know:

For though I knew His love who followed
Yet was I sore adread
Lest, having Him, I must have naught beside.

The strange fear of many is that in choosing God we surrender other desirable things—that in commitment to him we give up freedom—whereas in fact our greatest freedom comes only in total commitment to God. And with freedom comes wholeness and happiness. "Daughter, thy faith hath made thee whole." (Mark 5:34.)

I love the word of a strong, noble woman: "Being single has its good and bad moments. Certainly it's a human experience, and that's what we all opted for."

And I love Tolstoi's story "The Candle" in which a peasant Russian, forced to plough on Easter, lighted a candle to his Lord and kept it burning on his plough as he worked through the sacred day.

There are many who light their candles and follow the plough, and among the noblest and bravest and most Christlike of them are many single adult women, worthy daughters of God. Their challenge and their decision are like that of Michael Collins, astronaut, pilot of the command craft that landed men on the moon and circled that distant orb waiting to rendezvous with them again and bring them safely home. He did not land with his companions who walked on the moon, but flew alone in the spacecraft while they made their first long step. Afterward he wrote:

"It is perhaps a pity that my eyes have seen more than my brain has been able to assimilate or evaluate.

"But, like the Druids of Stonehenge, I have attempted to bring order out of what I have observed, even if I have not understood it fully.

"I have no intention of spending the rest of my life looking backward—There is magic aplenty for me here on earth."

WHY EVERY WOMAN NEEDS RELIEF SOCIETY

Elder Mark E. Petersen

The prophet Joshua was a great leader in ancient Israel. He probably is best known for the thrilling challenge he gave to his people as he said: "Choose you this day whom ye will serve; . . . as for me and my house, we will serve the Lord." (Joshua 24:15.)

This challenge now faces us also in stern reality. Worldliness is increasing at a frightening rate. I do not speak of sin and corruption alone. I speak also of worldly philosophies and ideologies that now compete with the gospel for our acceptance and adoption. We are too prone to accept the wisdom of the world rather than the humble advice of leaders of the Church. Highly sophisticated planners in important governmental or educational fields seem, to some people, to speak with greater authority and relevance than the prophets of God.

As we listen more and more to these individuals, we tend to listen less and less to our inspired Church leaders. We compare the two—the highly educated experts and the humble men who guide our religious thoughts. Too often this results in a cooling of attitudes of some individuals toward the Church, with an accompanying transfer of loyalties.

But now is the time to reassess our selection of values. Now is the time to remind ourselves that God has restored his gospel and that it is given to us as a way of life—our way of life—God's way of life. We must awaken to the realization that if we are going to truly serve the Lord, we must put the Church and the gospel first in our lives and not allow worldly philosophies to crowd them out or to downgrade them.

Hence we must reassert to ourselves the challenge of Joshua: "Choose you this day whom ye will serve." Shall we follow the ways of men, or shall we follow the prophets?

We must never allow ourselves to forget that the Lord has restored his gospel and that we are his people. That restoration included the reestablishment of the Church of Jesus Christ with all its gifts and blessings. It returned to the earth the Lord's plan of salvation. The plan of salvation is implemented through the program of the Church, so for all practical purposes the program of the Church is the plan of salvation. It is the means—the vehicle, if you please—whereby we work out our salvation here on the earth.

If we engage in the program of the Church, we do work out our salvation. If we are not active in the program of the Church, we forfeit the blessings of salvation.

When the Prophet Joseph Smith organized and established the Church, he included in that organization the women's Relief Society. Do we realize the significance of that? Relief was made a part of the restored church by action of the great restorer, Joseph Smith. It was given to the women of the Church in Nauvoo, Illinois, during the formative period of the Church. It was intended to fill a great need. It was expected that it would be perpetuated down through the years. It was to accomplish certain specific ends. For example:

1. It was to make better Latter-day Saints of us all.

2. It was to build stronger homes.

3. It was to strengthen our marriages.

4. It was to help us rear stronger Latter-day Saint children.

5. It was to help us make the Golden Rule function better among us as we render compassionate service to others.

6. It was to strengthen our communities and make our neighborhoods better places in which to live.

7. It was to educate our sisters in successful ways to solve their personal problems.

8. It was to give them an appreciation of good literature and other cultural advantages to enrich and broaden their lives.

9. It was to help our women see their inspired role in life as partners with God in the high estate of wives and mothers.

10. It was to help our sisters to know that Mormon women are not second-class citizens, that they are not confined and circumscribed, and that they need not look for liberation in the avenues of the world.

Mormon women in their true setting as handmaidens of the Lord are the freest women on earth. They have the greatest opportunity for self-expression and service to others of any women in the world. Why? Because they have the gospel.

The apostle Paul taught the Corinthians that wherever the Spirit of the Lord is, there is liberty. (See 2 Corinthians 3:17.) And the Book of Mormon says that the Spirit of God is the spirit of freedom. (See Alma 61:15.)

Through the gospel, then, we can bring a new birth of freedom to the women of the Church. But they must be brought into the gospel—into activity in the Church—in order to enjoy it. Hence we must do all within our power to enlist their activity within our ranks so that they may really taste of the sweet fruits of God's version of liberation. He can provide liberty and justice for all.

The gospel elevates womankind like nothing else can. It puts our sisters on a pedestal. They become queens in their homes. As daughters of God, they can become like God, and is there any greater goal in life? The gospel teaches us to become perfect like him. As children of our Heavenly Father, is it not our destiny to become like him?

And by what means are we to do so?

Paul taught the Ephesians that the Church organization is for the perfecting of the Saints. (See Ephesians 4.) Therefore, it is only through the Church that we can reach our greatest goals.

The Lord has given us priesthood quorums for the men and boys. He has given us the Primary for the children and the Sunday School for us all, wherein we may learn the doctrines of the Church. He has given us organizations for girls and young adults. And for the women of the Church he has given us the Relief Society. This great organization is devoted wholeheartedly to the interests of women. It is the Lord's organization especially provided for them.

I remind you that the program of the Church is the plan of salvation and that Relief Society is a part of that plan. It is God-given. It is inspired. It will lift everyone who participates in it. It is part and parcel of the Lord's program for the Church, and therefore every woman should come within its divine influence.

The apostle Paul taught that all parts of the body or Church of Christ are essential. The hand cannot say to the feet, "I have no need of thee." (1 Corinthians 12:21.) Neither can the priesthood say to the Relief Society, "I have no need of thee." Nor can the Sunday School, nor the Primary. All parts—fitly joined together—are needed for the perfecting of the Saints.

Would the Church be complete without the priesthood, or without the Primary or Sunday School? Could perfection come to the Saints without them? Then would the Church be complete without the Relief Society? And is it not a part of the process by which perfection comes to the Saints?

Inasmuch, then, as Relief Society is the inspired and God-given organization for the women of the Church, is it not needed by *every* Latter-day Saint woman? What Mormon woman can say to the Relief Society, "I have no need of thee"?

Are we to set aside the counsel and plan of God? Are we to prefer the way of man over the way of God? Or are we to ignore both and merely content ourselves with living in the darkness of isolated privacy?

Relief Society is vital to the welfare of every Latter-day Saint woman. But more than that, it is also essential to the welfare of every Latter-day Saint family. Otherwise, why would the Almighty have made it an integral part of his modern kingdom?

Since the Relief Society program will benefit the entire family, the whole family should support it and encourage all sisters to participate in it. Children should *want* their mothers to attend and learn how to be better mothers. And certainly fathers, of all people, should earnestly desire their wives to become a part of this great organization. Husbands should even selfishly desire this in the interest of better homemaking, of improving the atmosphere of the home, and of increasing its efficiency. But especially should fathers support it as a means of bringing into the family circle that portion of the restored kingdom of God which is available only through the Relief Society. Every husband and father should actually sponsor the attendance of his wife in Relief Society. It should be a "must" in every household.

We have no right to turn our backs on any part of the Lord's kingdom, and certainly not in exchange for the philosophies and ideologies and organizations of the world. We in the Church must remember that we are under covenant to seek first the kingdom of God and his righteousness.

The ways of men are not God's ways. The Lord has said that the wisdom of men is often foolishness to him. Revelation is a better guide than human research or speculation.

Remembering the part the Prophet Joseph Smith took in forming the Relief Society, how can we sing "We thank thee, O God, for a prophet to guide us in these latter days" (*Hymns*, no. 196) if we are not willing to follow the prophet's direction? It is not our privilege to choose what part or portion of the gospel we will live. The Lord expects us to accept and live it all—wholeheartedly!

Brilliant men have tried to stem the tide of retrogression in our modern society. They recite frightening statistics about the erosion of the home, the break-down of morals, and our ever-increasing dishonesty.

Are you shocked to learn that there are more than 2,000 divorces a week in the United States? Are you pained to know that three million children in America are financially destitute after having experienced family disruption with all of its evils? Eight million children in America live with only one parent. Another million have been rejected by both parents. Forty million American husbands and wives need help in solving their marriage problems. Twenty million homes are in trouble. Eighty percent of all delinquent children say they receive little or no love or guidance from their parents, who neglect them, reject them, and are cruel to them.

The rapid breakdown of the home and family in America is appalling. All of the efforts of our well-trained intellectuals cannot stem the tide. Their efforts for the most part have met with failure.

Then should we not now turn to God and his plan? It is certain. It is sure. It is successful. Should we not endeavor to place in every Latter-day Saint home the safeguards offered by the program of the Church—the whole program, including the Relief Society? Certainly in the Church, of all places, we should not allow man's failing ways to displace God's ways. And neither can any of us continue to ignore God's way of doing things. The times are critical. They demand our obedience. If we believe in God, let us prove our faith by our works.

Many women do not attend Relief Society. They have not yet seen the opportunity it affords. They have not yet learned that Relief Society is given to us to help solve many of the problems that are now baffling the women of today.

The full import of the restored gospel seems not yet to have dawned upon them. This is more regrettable since it is only through this gospel that we may truly serve the Lord and receive his blessings, and his blessings will bring us peace. And keep in mind that Relief Society is a part of his program.

So now, sisters, you must help to bring every Latter-day Saint woman into this organization. And with them, bring their nonmember friends. All are welcome.

Counsel with the priesthood leaders in your homes. Obtain their help in urging the brethren to encourage their wives and older daughters to come. Then we ask you to labor with the women of your areas. Do not be content merely with inviting them to come. Go to them as missionaries. Show them, demonstrate to them, teach them what Relief Society will do for them. Become their friends. Fellowship them regularly and constantly.

One of the areas in which we are most lacking as a people is that of fellowshipping. Paul taught anciently that all saints should be fellowshipped and made to feel that they are fellow citizens in the kingdom and that they are truly of the household of God. (See Ephesians 2:19.) People need this sense of belonging. Everybody needs it. Some have left the Church because they have not been given this feeling. They have not truly felt welcome. Some have been ignored by other members. That is not the spirit of the gospel. It is not the way to promote activity in the Church.

By our friendly spirit, by our adoption of Paul's teaching, by our truly regarding all Saints as fellow citizens in the kingdom and as members of the household of God, whether they are active or inactive, newcomers or members of long standing—I say, by such an attitude we can and will save many souls.

Many know nothing of the Relief Society program. If they knew the facts, they would see what a help Relief Society would be to them. Let them see how our work will enrich their homes and their personal lives. Show them the value of making new friends and companionships among the women who now come. If properly approached, they will be complimented by your attention to them. Most of them will be opened to conversion. Most women are good women, and good women need the companionship of others like themselves.

Be Relief Society missionaries. As you do so, you will be as saviors on Mount Zion to thousands. Their souls are precious; their families are precious in the sight of God. As you bring in these women, you may be bringing salvation to their entire households.

So, sisters, as a means of saving souls and strengthening families, let us endeavor to bring every woman to Relief Society. Do not make this a one-time effort. It should be a continuing project with each of us. The Good Shepherd did not spare any effort to bring home the lost sheep. Neither should we. May we follow his example and truly be his helpers on Mount Zion.

BEGIN WHERE YOU ARE— AT HOME

Elder Boyd K. Packer

The following words are for Relief Society sisters whose husbands are not at present active in the Church or are not yet members of the Church.

Each weekend as we travel to stake conferences, we meet one or two stake leaders who have joined the Church after many years, through the encouragement of a patient and, not infrequently, long-suffering wife.

I have often said that a man cannot resist membership in the Church if his wife really wants him to have it, and if she knows how to give him encouragement. Frequently we give up on this matter. Now, you can't ever give up—not in this life or in the next. You can never give up.

Some have joined the Church after finding it at a very late hour in life or after lingering for many years before taking that step. Then comes the regret over the wasted years, and the question, "Why couldn't I have realized earlier? It is too late for me to learn the gospel or to progress in it."

I think we should take great comfort from the parable of the householder who hired laborers and set them to work at the first hour at an agreed price. Then he "found others standing idle, and saith unto them, Why stand ye here all the day idle? They say unto him, Because no man hath hired us. He saith unto them, Go ye also into the vineyard; and whatsoever is right, that shall ye receive."

And so it was, even to the eleventh hour, that he hired others and set them to work. And when the day was over he gave the same pay to every one of them. Those who had come early murmured, saying, "These last have wrought but one hour, and thou hast made them equal unto us, which have borne the burden and heat of the day."

And the Lord said to them, "Friend, I do thee no wrong: didst not thou agree with me for a penny? Take that thine is, and go thy way: I will give unto this last, even as unto thee. Is it not lawful for me to do what I will with mine own?" (Matthew 20:6-15.)

He wasn't talking about money.

The gates of the celestial kingdom will open to those who come early or late. Sisters, you must never give up. If you have faith enough and desire enough, you will yet have at the head of your home a father and a husband who is active and faithful in the Church.

Some who have long since lost hope have said bitterly, "It would take a miracle." And so I say, Why not? Why not a miracle? Is there a purpose more worthy than that?

At a conference in England I spoke to the sisters along this line and encouraged them to regard their husbands as though they were active members of the Church, and to do this with a gesture of faith that it might bring about the very thing they desired. Some time later I received a long letter from a sister who had attended that meeting. I include a sentence or two:

"In my patriarchal blessing," she says, "I was told that by gentle persuasion and guidance, teaching love and understanding, my husband will mellow toward the Church, and, given the opportunity, he will accept the gospel. He will find it difficult, but if he opens his heart and lets the Lord and the Holy Spirit work within him, then he will recognize the gospel and follow its course.

"I worried," she said, "because I am not always gentle, loving, and understanding, but more angry with him at times; and yet I knew that this was wrong. I prayed to the Lord to help me, and this help was spoken by you when you said that we were to treat our husbands as though they were members of the Church.

"This I have done these past few days and it has helped me tremendously, for if my husband held the holy priesthood of God, then I would be a more obedient wife and honor the priesthood. We have become closer, and I realize that unless I become gentle, loving, and understanding now, I am unworthy to be honored with the priesthood in my home."

Then this lovely sister added, with hope, "That my husband and I and our six children may be sealed in the holy temple and serve the Lord as a family united in Christ."

In order to help with a miracle like this, I would like to share some thoughts about what a man is and make suggestions as to how a woman might approach this challenge.

First, virtually every man knows that he should be giving righteous spiritual leadership in the home. The scriptures say very clearly that "men are instructed sufficiently that they know good from evil. . . ." (2 Nephi 2:5.)

Often, when a woman joins the Church before her husband does, or if she is a member of the Church when they marry, she readily becomes the spiritual leader in the family. The father then doesn't quite know how to step to her side, even though he may see this as his proper place. He somehow feels that he might be replacing her. Often a man will feel uncomfortable, hold back, resist, not knowing quite how to wrest that spiritual leadership from his wife.

There are some very delicate feelings related to this matter that involve the male ego and touch the very center of the nature of manhood. And I must say in all candor that not infrequently a woman can become so determined to lead her husband to activity in the Church that she fails to realize that she could let him lead her there very quickly.

Remember, dear sisters, that the home and the family are a unit of the Church. Once you recognize that fact, you will come to know, in a very real sense, that when you are at home you are at church, or at least you should be. Somehow we get set in our minds that a man is not active unless he is attending meetings regularly at the chapel. I recall President Harold B. Lee saying once that someone close to him, if judged by that term, was inactive, and yet he knew him to be a saintly man. But the mere act of a man's leaving home and going to the meetinghouse is somehow thought of as a symbol of his activity in the Church.

This, then, often becomes the first thing we try to do—get him to attend meetings at the chapel—when generally this is not the beginning at all. That happens later. Now let me make this suggestion.

It is difficult to get a man to go to church when he doesn't feel at home there. It may be new and different to him, or perhaps there are habits he has not yet overcome, and he may feel self-conscious and just not feel at home at church. There is another solution, you know—that of making him feel as if he's at church while at home.

We often don't properly credit what he does at home. It's that going to the chapel that gets fixed in our minds as the symbol of church activity. But in many ways the things he does at home can be more important as a beginning.

And so this suggestion: Why don't you begin where you are, right at home? And I repeat, if your husband doesn't feel at home going to church, then do everything you can to make him feel at church while he's at home.

How can you do this? The Relief Society can answer that. To me the greatest challenge before Relief Society in our day is that of assisting our lovely sisters to provoke their husbands to good works.

Recently a study was completed involving families with inactive or nonmember fathers. These fathers agreed, after some persuasion, to institute the family home evening program in their homes. Gradually they were drawn into participation. This program had appeal because it was conducted in their own comfortable environment, and they could do it pretty much as they wished—the family home evening program is just that adaptable. There was an interesting result to this experiment. When the fathers felt comfortable with the Church at home, then they began to go to church with their families.

To bring some of the things of heaven into the home is to insure that family members will graduate to church participation. The family home evening is, of course, ready-made for this—a meeting at home that can be organized to fit every need; and it is just as much a church meeting, or can be, as those held at the chapel.

It may take a miracle for your husband to become active or to join the Church. Some of us think a miracle is a miracle only if it happens instantly, but miracles can grow slowly. And patience and faith can compel things to happen that otherwise never would have come to pass. It took a sister of mine seventeen years of patience, but it was well worth it. I knew a bishop who took thirty years to become active. He said he didn't believe in rushing into things.

So begin where you are, in the home, and have patience, whether it takes a little while, or a long while, or nearly an eternity. There is a meaningful scripture in the book of Ether: ". . . dispute not because ye see not, for ye receive no witness until after the trial of your faith." (Ether 12:6.)

Building a heaven in your home will do much to make these miracles.

One family in the previously cited survey, when visited after a few months of having family home evening, was asked, "Did you have family home evening every week?" The wife replied, "We don't know. There was one week when we don't know whether we had family home evening or not." She was asked, "What did you do?" With tears in her eyes she said, "That's the night our family went to the temple to be sealed together."

The husband, who was now a Melchizedek Priesthood holder, sat straight in his chair and was filled with joy as he related how family home evening had caused them to sense the true importance of family life and the need for spirituality.

The wife explained, "The night we went to the temple was my birthday. I didn't get a present because now that we are paying tithing, we don't have any extra money." Then she looked at her husband and said, "The greatest present I ever received from you was the night you took us all to the temple."

Another woman said of her husband, "The best family home evenings we had were when my husband taught." As the husband heard this he said, "Oh, I didn't do so good." She said, "Oh, but you did. I was really proud of you."

Then he said (and isn't this like a man?), "I guess I did do pretty good. You know, I've always been a black sheep, but when I taught my own family, I got a feeling that I had never had before, and everything seemed to make sense." And now this man comes over to the chapel and is active there. It all started with church at home.

Now if the husband does not, in the beginning, hold up his end of making miracles, and he probably won't, then you do your part all the better. Make the gospel seem so worthwhile that he can't resist it.

Some years ago Elder A. Theodore Tuttle and I called to see a local leader of the Church in the early evening before going on to another city. He had not arrived home from work, and his wife was busy in the kitchen. She invited us to sit at the kitchen table and visit while she continued her work. Box lunches were set on the counter. She explained that there was to be a box supper at the branch that night and she had spent the whole day preparing the finest lunches she could.

About the time her husband arrived, she took from the oven some hot cherry pies. Being a hospitable woman, she insisted that we share the hot cherry pie smothered in ice cream. Of course, we did not resist.

She then glanced at her husband, and I could tell what she was thinking: "He'd like a piece of pie too, but it will dull his appetite for the box supper later. It isn't kind to have him sit and watch them eat, but if he eats he won't enjoy the meal I've worked so hard to prepare."

Finally this silent argument in her mind was ended and she cut another piece of pie—noticeably bigger than the ones we had, with just a little bit more ice cream. She set it on the table before him, slipped her hands down under his chin, squeezed him just a little, and said, "Honey, it kind of makes the gospel seem worthwhile, doesn't it?"

Later when I teased her a little bit about spoiling him that way, she said, "He'll never leave me. I know how to treat a man."

I repeat—the greatest challenge facing Relief Society in our day is to help the lovely wives of these hundreds of thousands of men to encourage their husbands and to make a heaven in their homes. Sisters, make the gospel seem worthwhile to them, and then let them know that that is your purpose.

Most women expect men to perceive those things, and become irritated and sometimes upset when they don't. But men just aren't that sensitive. A man can be thick-skulled, dull-witted, and unconscious sometimes when it comes to things like this. When you say to yourself, or to another, "Well, he ought to know what it is I want most," perhaps he *ought* to know, but he probably doesn't, and he needs to be told.

I was told once of a home teacher trying to encourage the father to pray in the home. The father resisted and sat down on the couch. Finally he knelt but wouldn't pray. His wife was then invited to pray, and through her tears she poured out her heart to the Lord, pleading with him for what she wanted most. When the prayer was over, this husband, a startled man—and, I think, in many ways an innocent man—said, "I didn't know that. I didn't know that was what you wanted. You're going to see some changes in me."

Your husband needs to know, he needs to be told,

that you care about the gospel as deeply as you do and that you care about him infinitely more because of the gospel and what it means to you. Let him know that your goodness as a wife and as a mother, as a sweetheart and as a companion in love, grows from your testimony of the gospel.

Now I want to speak briefly to you lovely sisters who are left alone. I should rephrase that, I think, for no one is left alone. I refer to those of you who have not had the privilege of marriage or who have lost your husbands through the tragedy of divorce or perhaps through the inevitable call of death.

Some of you are struggling to raise little families alone, often on meager budgets and often with hours of loneliness. I know there is a great power of compensation. I know there is a spirit that can give you power to be both father and mother, if necessary.

There stands in our small circle of General Authorities more than one man who was raised in the home of an attentive, lovely widowed mother. I heard one of them bear testimony in conference that in his boyhood days they had all the things that money couldn't buy.

There is a priesthood shelter, sisters, under which you come. There is the bishop who stands as the father of the ward. Let him help, and the others he may delegate. Let your home teacher assist, particularly when you need the influence of manhood in the raising of boys.

Remember, you are not alone. There is a Lord who loves you, and he watches over you, and there is the power of the Spirit that can compensate.

And so, to you also, I say, you must never give up. Never, neither in this world nor in the next. For there comes a time when the judgments are rendered, and as the Lord said in that parable, ". . . whatsoever is right I will give you." (Matthew 20:4.)

There is an interesting scripture in Alma: ". . . behold I say unto you, that by small and simple things are great things brought to pass; and small means in many instances doth confound the wise." (Alma 37:6.)

So here is a Relief Society sister, a lovely mother, with a spoon and a bowl, with an apron and a broom, with a pie tin, a mixer, a cookie cutter, and a skillet, with a motherly gesture, with patience, with long-suffering, with affection, with a needle and thread, with a word of encouragement, with that bit of faith and determination to build an ideal home. With all of these small things you and the Relief Society can win for yourselves, and for The Church of Jesus Christ of Latter-day Saints, and for the Lord, the strength and power of a family knit together, sealed together for time and for all eternity; a great army of men, some willing and worthy, some not yet worthy, but who must serve in the ministry of our Lord; men who now stand by the sidelines—husbands and fathers not quite knowing, some not quite willing, yet all to be strengthened by a handmaiden of the Lord who really cares.

May God bless you, sisters. May he bless you who are the widows and the others who are rearing families alone everywhere. May he bless you hundreds of thousands of wives and mothers who through the agency of the Relief Society now can be strengthened to the end that your dreams might be realized.

SCRIPTURES AND FAMILY STABILITY

President Marion G. Romney

At the heart of society's fatal sickness is the instability of the family. Being conscious of this and concerned about it, may I point out how the scriptures relate to family stability.

Perhaps an accurate short example would be to say that the scriptures relate to the stability of a family much the same as a set of working drawings and specifications relates to a building.

When a building is constructed, before ground is broken for that structure, every detail thereof, from subsoil to tower pinnacle, must be considered, planned, and drawn out. Specifications covering in detail all labor and material requirements must be reduced to writing. A study must be made to determine how strong the steel to be used must be in order to withstand earthquake shock and wind pressure. The completed plans and specifications must be submitted to and considered by the contractors as they bid the job. In the construction of the building, these plans must be meticulously followed.

From the scriptures we learn that the Lord himself, before creating the earth, planned all things pertaining thereto in detail.

". . . I, the Lord God, made the heaven and the earth;

"And every plant of the field before it was in the earth, and every herb of the field before it grew. For I, the Lord God, created all things, of which I have spoken, spiritually, before they were naturally upon the face of the earth. . . ." (Moses 3:4-5.)

Now, families are of infinitely more worth than buildings. They are of more worth than the earth itself. The Lord has said that all his creations, including the earth, are calculated to aid in his great work, "to bring to pass the immortality and eternal life of man." (Moses 1:39.) He has further revealed the fact that no man can gain eternal life except as a member of an enduring and stable family. This being so, it is inconceivable that God would not have a plan and specifications for building the family, his most precious and enduring creation. The fact is, he did have such a plan and specifications. Both are set forth in the scriptures.

To understand and follow God's plans and specifications for building families is as essential to the building of stable and enduring families as is understanding and following plans and specifications for material buildings and planets. That God's plans and specifications for the building of families are not understood and followed accounts in large measure for the instability of the family in modern society.

The scriptures reveal the fact that the family is a divine and not a man-made institution. They make it clear that God is the literal Father of a great family to which all the inhabitants of the earth belong; that the spirits of men are his begotten sons and daughters; that his work and his glory is to bring them to that perfection and exaltation which he himself enjoys. The scriptures explain that in order for them to obtain such perfection, they must be tabernacled in physical bodies of flesh and bone and then be proved in a mortal probation.

God's plan for the accomplishment of this objective provided for his spirit children to be clothed in mortal bodies and then be united as husbands and wives by the power of his holy priesthood; that so wedded, they were to be, while in mortality, under divine covenant to multiply and replenish the earth—that is, to provide mortal bodies for others of God's spirit children and thus assist him in bringing to pass their eternal life.

The plan provided that couples so married would in eternity persist as husbands and wives, and would there progress until they eventually reached perfection and themselves became parents of spirit children.

Such was the plan designed by the Lord for families before the foundations of this earth were laid.

To implement this great plan, "God created man in his own image . . . male and female." (Genesis 1:27.) Not only were they created in form, but he also joined them—after the order of his own marital status—in holy wedlock as husband and wife for eternity. Having done so, he commanded them to "be fruitful, and multiply, and replenish the earth." (Genesis 1:28.)

The idea that marriage is a man-made social custom that may be done away with at will is of the evil one. Not only is marriage God-ordained: his plan also calls for it to be enduring, for it must be for the building of stable and enduring families.

The Pharisees came to Jesus and asked him, "Is it lawful for a man to put away his wife?

"And he answered and said unto them, What did Moses command you?

"And they said, Moses suffered to write a bill of divorcement, and to put her away.

"And Jesus answered and said unto them, For the hardness of your heart he wrote you this precept.

"But from the beginning of the creation God made them male and female.

"For this cause shall a man leave his father and mother, and cleave to his wife;

"And they twain shall be one flesh: so then they are no more twain, but one flesh.

"What therefore God hath joined together, let not man put asunder.

"And in the house his disciples asked him again of the same matter.

"And he saith unto them, Whosoever shall put away his wife, and marry another, committeth adultery against her.

"And if a woman shall put away her husband, and be married to another, she committeth adultery." (Mark 10:2-12.)

If the teachings of Jesus as they are found in the Bible were followed, honorable marriage would be the objective of all men and there would be no divorce. This would eliminate a major cause of family instability.

In addition to what Jesus taught about marriage and divorce, there is much additional scripture. Some things Paul said about marriage are, as Peter said, a bit "hard to be understood" (2 Peter 3:16), but concerning the separation of husband and wife he spoke clearly and with emphasis. Having been directed by the Lord, he said: ". . . unto the married I command, yet not I, but the Lord, Let not the wife depart from her husband: But and if she depart, let her remain unmarried, or be reconciled to her husband: and let not the husband put away his wife." (1 Corinthians 7:10-11.)

The utterances of modern prophets on the subject of marriage and divorce are in full harmony with the Bible scriptures. As to marriage, the Prophet Joseph received the following revelations: ". . . verily I say unto you, that whoso forbiddeth to marry is not ordained of God, for marriage is ordained of God unto man." (D&C 49:15.)

President Brigham Young is quoted as saying on April 6, 1845: "I tell you the truth as it is in the bosom of eternity; and I say so to every man upon the face of the earth: if he wishes to be saved he cannot be saved without a woman by his side." (Times and Seasons 6:955.)

President Joseph F. Smith declared: "I want the young men of Zion to realize that this institution of marriage is not a man-made institution. It is of God. It is honorable, and no man who is of marriageable age is living his religion who remains single. . . . Marriage is the preserver of the human race. Without it, the purposes of God would be frustrated; virtue would be destroyed to give place to vice and corruption, and the earth would be void and empty." (Gospel Doctrine, p. 272.)

In our consideration of the Lord's overall plan, his purpose for the institution of enduring marriage was propagation: the bringing of God's spirit children into mortal life. The scriptures are as specific on this point as they are concerning marriage and divorce.

"Wherefore, it is lawful that [a man] should have one wife, and they twain shall be one flesh, and all this that the earth might answer the end of its creation;

"And that it might be filled with the measure of man, according to his creation before the world was made." (D&C 49:16-17).

In another scripture, the Lord says that wives are given unto men "to multiply and replenish the earth, according to my commandment, and to fulfil the promise which was given by my Father before the foundation of the world, and for their exaltation in the eternal worlds, that they may bear the souls of men; for herein is the work of my Father continued, that he may be glorified." (D&C 132:63.)

I can think of no more profound and glorious scripture than this, which declares the purpose of marriage to be, first, that the earth "might be filled with the measure of man, according to his creation before the world was made," thereby continuing the work of the Father "that he may be glorified"; and second, that men may obtain for themselves "exaltation in the eternal worlds" according to the promise given by the Father before the foundation of the world.

With this divine concept of marriage, divorce, and the bearing of children in mind, it is easy to understand the following statements of the modern prophets.

From President Brigham Young: "There are multitudes of pure and holy spirits waiting to take tabernacles, now what is our duty?—To prepare tabernacles for them; to take a course that will not tend to drive those spirits into the families of the wicked, where they will be trained in wickedness, debauchery, and every species of crime. It is the duty of every righteous man and woman to prepare tabernacles for all the spirits they can." (*Discourses of Brigham Young*, p. 197.)

With respect to birth control, President Joseph F.

Smith said, in 1917: "I regret, I think it is a crying evil, that there should exist a sentiment or a feeling among any members of the Church to curtail the birth of their children. I think that is a crime wherever it occurs, where husband and wife are in possession of health and vigor and are free from impurities that would be entailed upon their posterity. I believe that where people undertake to curtail or prevent the birth of their children that they are going to reap disappointment by and by. I have no hesitancy in saying that I believe this is one of the greatest crimes of the world today, this evil practice." (*Gospel Doctrine*, pp. 278-79.)

On these matters, the First Presidency has said: "We have given careful consideration to the question of proposed laws on abortion and sterilization. We are opposed to any modification, expansion, or liberalization of laws on these vital subjects." (Letter to stake presidents in the state of Washington, October 27, 1970.)

The following are samples of the many other scriptures that materially relate to family stability:

"Train up a child in the way he should go: and when he is old, he will not depart from it." (Proverbs 22:6.)

"And, ye fathers, provoke not your children to wrath: but bring them up in the nurture and admonition of the Lord." (Ephesians 6:4.)

King Benjamin counseled parents not to "suffer your children that they go hungry, or naked; neither will ye suffer that they transgress the laws of God, and fight and quarrel one with another, and serve the devil. . . . But ye will teach them to walk in the ways of truth and soberness; ye will teach them to love one another, and to serve one another." (Mosiah 4:14-15.)

". . . I have commanded you to bring up your children in light and truth." (D&C 93:43.)

Children have obligations to their parents: "Children, obey your parents in the Lord: for this is right. Honour thy father and mother; . . . That it may be well with thee, and thou mayest live long on the earth." (Ephesians 6:1-3.)

And husbands and wives have obligations to each other: "Wives, submit yourselves unto your own husbands, as it is fit in the Lord. Husbands, love your wives, and be not bitter against them." (Colossians 3:18-19.)

Compliance with these scriptures will do much toward stabilizing families.

I desire to call attention to some of the scriptural instructions on one more subject, that of prayer. I can think of no subject of which the scriptures speak more frequently, nor can I think of any practice that will do more to promote family stability.

The first recorded communication between mortal man and God resulted from prayer. The scriptures say that some time after they had been driven from the garden, "Adam and Eve, his wife, called upon the name of the Lord, and they heard the voice of the Lord from the way toward the Garden of Eden, speaking unto them. . . . And he gave unto them commandments, that they should worship the Lord their God. . . ." (Moses 5:4-5.)

From then until now, the scriptures have repeatedly admonished us to pray. The psalmist sang: "As for me, I will call upon God; and the Lord shall save me. Evening, and morning, and at noon, will I pray, and cry aloud: and he shall hear my voice." (Psalm 55:16-17.)

From Amulek's classic call to pray, recorded in the thirty-fourth chapter of Alma, I quote the following: "Cry unto him in your houses, yea, over all your household, both morning, midday, and evening. . . . But this is not all; ye must pour out your souls in your closets, and your secret places, and in your wilderness. Yea, and when you do not cry unto the Lord, let your hearts be full, drawn out in prayer unto him continually for your welfare, and also for the welfare of those who are around you." (Alma 34:21, 26-27.)

Jesus prayed by himself; he prayed with his disciples; he prayed for them. He instructed them to pray and gave them a prayer pattern.

The Prophet Joseph Smith's first vision, which

opened up this last dispensation, came in answer to prayer.

Two years before the Church was organized, the Lord gave this instruction: "Pray always, that you may come off conqueror; yea, that you may conquer Satan, and that you may escape the hands of the servants of Satan that do uphold his work." (D&C 10:5.)

At the time the Church was organized the Lord told the priesthood to "visit the house of each member, and exhort them to . . . attend to all family duties." The very first duty he specified was to "pray vocally and in secret." (D&C 20:47.)

Yes, God has a plan for building family stability, and that plan is revealed in the scriptures. May the Lord help all of us to implement that plan.

INDEX

Abortion, 96, 145
Adam, 14, 33-34; premortal
    identity of, 58-59; was created
    in immortality, 61; life of, after
    fall, 64-65; to preside at
    Adam-ondi-Ahman, 65-66;
    marriage of, 69-70, 80; prayed
    to God, 146. *See also* Fall of
    Adam
Addison, Joseph, 111
Alcohol, 5
Angels, ministering, 45
Armor of God, 77
Arnold, Matthew, 119
Ashton, Marvin J., chapter by,
    86-93
Astronaut, 122
Atonement, 57-58
Attitude, 111, 119-20
Auxiliary organizations of Church,
    2-4. *See also* Relief Society

Ballard, Melvin J., 114
Baten, Anderson M., 44
Benson, Ezra Taft, chapter by,
    69-76
Bible, women in, 95
Birth control, 145
Blessings: are not denied to single
    women, 113-14; are not
    automatic, 114; depend on
    attitude, 119-20
Body: care of, 108-11; Paul's
    analogy of, 126
Brave new world, 119
Brown, Hugh B., 7-8
Building, construction of, 140

C's, the three, 111
"Candle, The," 122

Carter, Jimmy, 23
Cherry pie, 136-37
Child abuse, 15, 35
Childhood memories, 107
Children: mothers' responsibilities
    toward, 6-7, 18; reading with,
    16; resurrection of, 43; have
    lost their place in society, 54;
    responsibility of bearing, 54,
    144; families not blessed with,
    54-55, 97; place of, in family,
    82; must be taught
    righteousness, 84-85, 145; in
    one-parent families, 115-16;
    delinquent, 128; obligations of,
    to parents, 145
Christie, Agatha, 119
Church of Jesus Christ of
    Latter-day Saints: auxiliary
    organizations of, 2-4; direction
    provided by, 9; does not
    restrict women's development,
    38-39; is not subject to man's
    will, 56; problems of marrying
    outside, 100-101; is family
    oriented, 101; must come
    before world, 123; programs of,
    implement plan of salvation,
    124, 126; purpose of, in
    perfecting Saints, 125;
    membership in, wives can
    encourage husbands to accept,
    131; home is unit of, 133;
    activity in, begins at home,
    134-35
Civilization, 36-37
Cleanliness, 111
Closet, child locked in, 105
Collins, Michael, 122
Communication of expectations,
    137-38
Community involvement: is

149

secondary to home
responsibilities, 11; of women
today, 87, 92-93
Compassionate service, 1, 3, 95.
See also Service
Concentration camp, survivor of,
106
Cotton gin, 89
Cow, keeping of, teaches
responsibility, 13
Crabb, Kelly, poem by, 30-31
Creation, 57-58; spiritual, 140
Credit explosion, 47

Daniel, 66
Death, sting of, 44
Divorce, 100, 115-18, 128, 142-43
Durham, G. Homer, chapter by,
32-40
Durrant, Will, 121

Earth: purpose of, 8; new, and new
heaven, 42-43; creation of, 59;
renewal of, 65; to be filled with
measure of man, 144
Eating habits, 110
Economy, national, 91
Edar, Dr. Jeanne, 90-91
Eden, 58, 59
Education, women should gain, in
many fields, 37, 86
Educational institutions, home is
greatest of, 34
Elect women, 69
Eleventh hour, laborers hired at,
131-32
Elisabeth, 95
Empathy, 96
Englemann, Siegfried and Therese,
23
Environment: influence of, 22-23;
pressure exerted by, 110
Equality between men and
women, 71
Eskimos, 36
Eternity: three most important
events in, 57-58; lends meaning
to time, 103-4

Evans, Richard L., 18-19
Eve: accepted responsibility of
motherhood, 14, 80-81; labored
alongside Adam, 33; in
premortal life, 58-59; role of, in
fall of man, 63-64; life of, after
fall, 64-65; verse about, 67; role
of, in plan of salvation, 67-68;
marriage of, 69-70, 80
Exaltation, 102, 144
Exercise: physical, 108, 109-10;
mental, 111-12

Faith, 104-5; trial of, 135
Fall of Adam: importance of,
57-58; plan of salvation
depended on, 61-62; Eve's role
in, 63-64. *See also* Adam
Family home evening, 9-10, 36,
134-36
Family organization: decline of, 32,
54, 128, 140; eternal nature of,
43-44, 51, 80, 141; father stands
at head of, 50-51, 133; threats
to, 92; Church emphasizes
importance of, 101; is benefited
by Relief Society, 127; is unit
of Church, 133; stability of,
role of scriptures in, 140; is part
of God's plan, 140-41;
scriptures pertaining to,
145-47. *See also* Home
Father: responsibilities of, 11-12,
36; death of, 13
Fellowshipping, 129
Fiddler on the Roof, 103
"First Christmas Story, The,"
30-31
Ford, Gerald R., 109-10
Foreordination of women, 94
Free agency, 103
Freedom: truth brings, 79; comes
from commitment to God, 122;
of Mormon women, 125

Gandhi, Mahatma, 120
Garden of Eden, 58, 59
Girls: importance of virtue in, 6;

influence of, on boys, 8; should prepare for temple marriage, 8; should prepare through education, 10-11

God: woman's partnership with, 4; entrusts his children to women, 17; created man in his image, 60, 80, 142; armor of, 77; total commitment to, 122; ways of, are not man's ways, 127; plan of, 140-41; is man's literal Father, 141

Godhood, potential to achieve, 2, 19, 33, 67

Gospel: restoration of, 124; brings freedom, 125; must be lived wholeheartedly, 127. *See also* Church of Jesus Christ of Latter-day Saints

Grayson, David, 112

Haight, David B., chapter by, 13-20

Hanks, Marion D., chapter by, 99-122

Happiness: depends on use of agency, 103; depends on attitude, 119-20; comes through unselfishness, 121

Heaven, new, and new earth, 42-43

Heavenly mother, 98

Helaman, stripling warriors of, 24

Helpmeet, man's need for, 41, 69

Heschel, Rabbi Abraham Joshua, 103

"Hole-in-the-Rock," 39

Home: success in, rests largely on gospel ideals, 2; righteousness in, 10; comes before community involvement, 11; is more than a building, 14-15; is greatest educational institution, 34; establishing of, is sacred responsibility, 46; likening of, to priesthood quorum, 52; factors enticing women away from, 89-90; appeals for preservation of, 91-92; community success begins in, 91-92; breakdown of, 128; is unit of Church, 133; church activity begins in, 134-35. *See also* Family organization

Home teachers, 116, 138

Hoover, Herbert, 9

Husbands: appreciation from, 4; should not be dictators, 11; responsibilities of, 12; wives' influence on, 27; relationship of, to wives, 52-53, 82-83; should encourage wives to attend Relief Society, 127; nonmember or inactive, 131-39

Identity crisis, 32

Indians, study of, 99

Industrial revolution, 89

Inflation, economic, 90

Inhibition, 121

Intelligence: glory of God is, 11, 37; contemporary challenges to, 32; Adam and Eve possessed, 33

International Congress of Women, 90

Isaiah, 42-43

Jesus Christ: purpose for mission of, 8-9; was taught by his mother, 30-31; relationship of, to church is as man and wife, 52-53; atonement of, 57; in premortal existence, 58-59; should be man's only master, 79; teachings of, on divorce, 142

John the Baptist, 120

Johnson, Samuel, 112

Jordan, David Starr, 120

Joshua, 123

Kimball, Camilla, 35-36, 97

Kimball, Spencer W.: introduction by, 1-3; on mother's presence when children came home, 17-18; on woman's potential,

33; chapter by, 77-85; dependence of, on wife, 97; on single women, 113

Laborers, parable of, 131-32
Leadership, 3; in home, 50, 133
Lee, Harold B., 12
Lee, Robert E., 24-25
Letter to daughter on eve of her marriage, 46-56
Life, definition of, 112
Loneliness, antidote for, 118
Love: environment of, 23; is necessary to survival, 107; lasts beyond death, 118-19; sublimation of, 121

Marriage: is ordained of God, 6, 143; first record of, 41; eternal, 44-45, 118-19, 141; poem about, 44; purpose of, 54, 143-44; of Adam and Eve, 69-70, 80; threats to, 80, 92; between Mormon and non-Mormon, 100-101
Mary, mother of Christ, 30-31, 59, 94-95
Mass media, 5, 78
Materialism, thrust toward, 47
Maxwell, Neal A., chapter by, 94-98
McConkie, Bruce R., chapter by, 57-68
McKay, David Lawrence, 29
McKay, David O., 24, 29, 71
Men: need women's support, 7; should live worthy of women's love, 11; stand at head of families, 50-51; can be insensitive, 137. See also Father; Husbands
Michael, 58-59
Millennium, state of children during, 43
Mind: and body, connections between, 108-9; needs exercise, 111-12

Miracles, 135
Missionary who wanted to go home, 27-28
Mormon, promise of, 105
Moses, 77-78
Mother: influence of, on children, 6-7, 23; creates atmosphere in home, 14-15, 22-23; teaching role of, 15-16, 21-22; prepares children to return to God, 17; presence of, when children come home, 17-18; cannot be substituted for, 19, 84; child calling for, in store, 19; sacrifices of, 22, 28-29; teaches by example, 25; faith of, in alcoholic husband, 26; raised nineteen children alone, 73; missionaries' appreciation for, 83. See also Motherhood; Wives
Motherhood: is woman's basic role, 13; involves many other roles, 14; necessary attributes of, 15, 35; requires time, 17-19; divine nature of, 19, 73, 84; is most exacting profession, 35, 38; connection of, with priesthood, 51. See also Mother
Multiply and replenish earth, 144
Music, 16-17, 25

Nature of man, 103
Neighbors, all men are, 106
"New Minority, The" 54
Niemoller, Martin, 106
Nutrition, 110

"O My Father," 81-82
Oaks, Dallin S., 5
Obedience, 120
"One flesh," man and woman should be, 41-42
Order in godly things, 48
Osborn, Dr. Anne G., 39-40

Packer, Boyd K., chapter by, 131-39

Index

Paramore, James M., chapter by, 46-56
Patience, 15, 135
Patriarchal order, 50-51
Paul, 44, 52-53, 83, 126
Petain, Henri, 106
Peter, 42
Petersen, Mark E., chapter by, 123-30
Physical exercise, 108, 109-10
Pie, 136-37
Pinegar, Rex D., chapter by, 21-31
Pioneer woman, determination of, 39
Plan of salvation, 8-9, 57, 61-62, 124, 141-42
Poirot, Hercule, 119
Pornography, 5
Possessions, becoming slaves to, 112
Prayer, 10, 17; of wife for inactive husband, 137; scriptural instructions on, 146-47
Priesthood, 50-52
Prisoners of war, conversation between, 8
Prophets, 48

Reading, 16, 111
Recreation, 111
Relief Society: organization of, 71-72; purposes of, 86-87, 124-25; importance of, to every woman, 126-27; benefits entire family, 127; inviting women to, 129-30
Resurrection of children, 43
Richards, LeGrand, chapter by, 41-45
Richards, Stephen L, 56
Righteousness, opposition against, 2
Romney, Marion G., chapter by, 140-47
Rose, a single perfect, 112
Ruth and Naomi, 94

Sacrifices of wives and mothers, 22, 28-29
Satan: efforts of, to destroy home and family, 5, 10; compromises with, are impossible, 8; distorts truth, 77; encounter of, with Moses, 77-78
Schiller, 21
Science, revolution in, 32
Scriptures: role of, in family stability, 140; examples of, pertaining to families, 145-47; instructions in, concerning prayer, 146-47
Self-image, 108
Self-pity, 106-7
Service: teaches godly qualities, 3; satisfaction in, 88; therapeutic value of, 105-8
Sex, 121
Shakespeare, 119
Single parents, 107-8, 115-16, 138
Single women, 97, 112-13, 138; quotations from, 99-101; faith of, 104-5; blessings are not withheld from, 113-14
Sleep, 110
Smith, Arabella, 39
Smith, Emma, 38, 69
Smith, Joseph, 72, 86, 121, 124
Smith, Joseph F., 86-87, 143, 145
Smith, Lucy Mack, 94
Socrates, 103
"Sons of Michael, He Approaches," 66-67
Spafford, Belle S., 87-89, 91
Stevenson, Robert Louis, 105
Suffrage, women's, 89-90

Tanner, N. Eldon, chapter by, 4-12
Teacher, unmarried, 114
Teaching: is a learning experience, 2-3; mother's role in, 15-16, 21-22
Technological revolution, 32, 90
Tempest, by Shakespeare, 119

Temple marriage, 8, 101, 135. *See also* Marriage
Thompson, Francis, 121
Thoreau, Henry David, 120
Thoughts, unworthy, 120
Time, motherhood requires, 17-19
Tolstoi, Leo, 105, 122
Truth makes men free, 79
Tuttle, A. Theodore, 136

Unisex, 92
Universities, comparison of homes to, 34
Unselfishness, 15, 95-96, 105-8
"Utah Women Speak," brochure, 91-92

Values, worldly, 47, 79, 123
Volunteer service, 92
Voting franchise, women should exercise, 93

Wells, Daniel H., 48-49
Wesley, John, 73
Wesley, Susannah, 73-74
Wheelchair, woman confined to, 109
Whitney, Eli, 89
Widows, 55, 95, 118-19
Widtsoe, John A., 50-51
Wives: influence of, on husbands, 27, 75; should sustain husbands in priesthood duties, 48-49; are subject to husbands, 52-53, 146; are preeminent in husbands' lives, 82; should follow husbands in righteousness, 83; childless, 97; men's dependence on, 97; should never give up on nonmember husbands, 131-32, 138-39. *See also* Mother; Motherhood

Women: influence of, in world, 1, 32; greatest potential of, 2, 33; work of, in Church auxiliaries, 2-3, 4; role of, in divine plan, 4, 9, 13-14, 50-51; primary responsibilities of, 6, 70; influence of, on men they love, 7-8; community involvement of, 11, 87, 92-93; blessings promised to, 12; basic role of, is motherhood, 13; influence of, on environment, 22-23; must discover their potential, 32; relationship of, to men, 33, 51-53; should qualify in two vocations, 35-36; should be well educated, 37, 77, 86; should feel needed, 40, 107; differences between men and, 69, 71, 94; in business world, 70-71; Joseph Smith's counsel to, 72; Paul's exhortations to, 83; should enlarge their sphere of usefulness, 86; in community life, 87; campaign of, for suffrage, 89-90; International Congress of, 90; serious-minded, need for, 93; should exercise voting franchise, 93; in Bible, 94-95; charity of, 95; unselfishness of, 95-96; unmarried, 97, 99-122; divorced, 100, 115-18; intrinsic worth of, 102; are elevated by gospel, 125. *See also* Mother; Motherhood; Wives
World: homage of, 4; values of, 47, 79, 123; wickedness of, was prophesied of, 48

Young, Brigham: on mothers, 7; on education, 37; on priesthood, 52; on childless women, 55; on Relief Society, 86; on marriage, 143; on bearing children, 144